Isaiah 56–66

BERIT OLAM
Studies in Hebrew Narrative & Poetry

Isaiah 56–66

Paul V. Niskanen

Chris Franke
Series Editor

A Michael Glazier Book

LITURGICAL PRESS
Collegeville, Minnesota

www.litpress.org

A Michael Glazier Book published by Liturgical Press

Cover design by Ann Blattner.

Unless otherwise noted, all translations from Scripture are the author's.

1   2   3   4   5   6   7   8   9

Library of Congress Cataloging-in-Publication Data

Niskanen, Paul.
    Isaiah 56–66 / Paul V. Niskanen.
        pages   cm. — (BERIT OLAM: studies in Hebrew narrative & poetry)
    "A Michael Glazier book."
    ISBN 978-0-8146-5068-4 — ISBN 978-0-8146-8256-2 (ebook)
    1. Bible. Isaiah, LVI–LXVI—Commentaries.   I. Title.

BS1520.5.N57   2014
224'.107—dc23   2014008292

CONTENTS

ABBREVIATIONS

AB	Anchor Bible
ABD	*Anchor Bible Dictionary.* Edited by D. N. Freedman. 6 vols. New York, 1992.
ANET	*Ancient Near Eastern Texts Relating to the Old Testament.* Edited by J. B. Pritchard. Princeton, 1954.
BDB	Brown, F., S. R. Driver, and C. A. Briggs. *A Hebrew and English Lexicon of the Old Testament.* Oxford, 1907.
BHS	*Biblia Hebraica Stuttgartensia.* Edited by K. Elliger and W. Rudolph. Stuttgart, 1983.
BTB	*Biblical Theology Bulletin*
BZAW	Beihefte zur Zeitschrift für die alttestamentliche Wissenschaft
CBQ	*Catholic Biblical Quarterly*
CD	Cairo Genizah copy of the *Damascus Document*
EBib	Etudes Bibliques
HeyJ	*Heythrop Journal*
HTR	*Harvard Theological Review*
IDBSup	*Interpreter's Dictionary of the Bible: Supplementary Volume.* Edited by K. Crim. Nashville, 1976.
JBL	*Journal of Biblical Literature*
JSJSup	Journal for the Study of Judaism Supplement
JSOT	*Journal for the Study of the Old Testament*
LXX	Septuagint
MT	Masoretic Text
NAB	New American Bible

NABRE	New American Bible Revised Edition
NCBC	New Century Bible Commentary
NIB	*The New Interpreter's Bible*
NIV	New International Version
NJPS	New Jewish Publication Society translation of the Tanakh
NRSV	New Revised Standard Version
OTL	Old Testament Library
OTM	Old Testament Message
PIBA	Proceedings of the Irish Biblical Association
RB	*Revue biblique*
SBL	Society of Biblical Literature
Syr	Syriac
Tg	Targum
Vg	Vulgate
VT	*Vetus Testamentum*
WBC	Word Biblical Commentary
WMANT	Wissenschaftliche Monographien zum Alten und Neuen Testament

INTRODUCTION

It is a somewhat peculiar enterprise to write a literarily focused commentary on Third Isaiah. There are, after all, no manuscripts of an independent literary composition known as Trito-Isaiah which one may examine, and the very recognition of Trito-Isaiah as a distinct unit within the book of Isaiah was not evident to anyone until the publication of Bernhard Duhm's commentary in 1892. Furthermore, the appearance of Third Isaiah in the world of scholarship with Duhm's commentary was the result of historical-critical as well as (or perhaps more than) literary considerations.[1] Duhm began by considering the different subject matter of chapters 56–66 compared to chapters 40–55. He found in the later chapters of Isaiah an interest in sacrifice and Sabbath observance that is absent in 40–55.[2] His initial observation, which can justly be called literary, quickly evolved into a historical argument for a later date (the middle of the fifth century BCE) and a different location (Palestine rather than Babylon) for chapters 56–66. So just as Isaiah 40–66 was first distinguished from Isaiah 1–39 by its easily discernible sixth-century historical context, so too, chapters 56–66 were further distinguished from chapters 40–55 as the postexilic Judean context of the former became

---

[1] Bernhard Duhm, *Das Buch Jesaja übersetzt und erklärt* (Göttingen: Vandenhoeck & Ruprecht, 1892).

[2] With the passage of time, it has also become more clear that the initial distinction between Second and Third Isaiah was made based on an unfortunate bias that saw an irreconcilable difference between "prophetic" and "priestly" concerns. The prophets were idealized by early modern scholars as representing the authentic religion of Israel over and against the cultic and legal concerns of priests and theocrats, which led to the devolution of prophetic religion into legalistic Judaism. This anti-Semitic reading of biblical history has had an unfortunate impact on biblical studies.

more clearly perceptible over and against the late exilic, Babylonian context of the latter.[3]

There is a very real danger of a type of circular argumentation here. If a work within a work (such as Trito-Isaiah within the book of Isaiah) is identified on the basis of subject matter and/or a plausible historical location for the composition of such subject matter, the very presuppositions behind the identification have a tendency to become the conclusive results of research. One can see this, for example, in the analysis of Isaiah 56–66 where passages that do not have an interest in sacrifice or Sabbath (e.g., 56:9–57:13) might be thought to be preexilic and therefore pre-Trito-Isaian.[4] One must be cautious when one knows an author only through that author's work, and yet that author's work is defined precisely according to what we believe we know about its author.

All of this does not mean, of course, that one cannot write a literary commentary on Third Isaiah. After all, the author(s) of each historically distinct part of the book of Isaiah would naturally have their own literary style and theological themes. What it does mean is that historical and literary studies of Scripture are more intimately linked than many practitioners of either would sometimes like to believe. It also means that I, at least, cannot undertake this commentary without acknowledging such connections and the necessary debt owed to scholars both historical and literary who have preceded me.

Another consideration that should be mentioned at the beginning of a commentary on Third Isaiah is the near-universal recognition that "it ain't that simple." That is to say, while commentaries continue to proceed along the now-traditional divisions of Isaiah 1–39, 40–55, and 56–66, few would actually maintain that these divisions are as clear as the volume titles would indicate. There is ample material in Isaiah 1–39 that shows evidence of composition or redaction by one or more of the

---

[3] Such distinctions are sometimes called into question today, especially with regard to the alleged Babylonian provenance of Second Isaiah. Lena-Sofia Tiemeyer has given an extensive argument for the Judean location of Isaiah 40–55 in *For the Comfort of Zion: The Geographical and Theological Location of Isaiah 40–55* (Leiden: Brill, 2011). I remain of the opinion, however, that such a geographical distinction is warranted at the very least by the location of the implied audience, but probably by the actual location as well, especially with respect to Isa 40–48. Since we are dealing here with Third rather than Second Isaiah, we need not enter into the debate concerning the latter's provenance. It is worth noting, however, that the implied geographical location of Trito-Isaiah is Zion and that its implied audience is the children of Zion who have returned (or are in the process of returning) there.

[4] So, e.g., Paul Volz, *Jesaia II, Kommentar zum alten Testament* (Leipzig: D. Werner Scholl, 1932), 207.

latter Isaiahs.[5] I myself have written concerning some of the "overlap" between Second and Third Isaiah.[6] And there are still champions of the authorial unity of Isaiah 40–66 today, over a century after Duhm's hypothesis was introduced.[7] So, on the one hand, biblical scholarship since Duhm has identified and distinguished a Trito-Isaiah within the book of Isaiah such that one may focus an analysis on the language, rhetoric, imagery, and theology of Isaiah 56–66 as the present work intends to do. Yet on the other hand, one is wise to recognize the connections as well as the distinctions. We are dealing not with an independent "book" but with a part of a larger work and so should keep this in sight as well while proceeding through chapters 56–66.

Looking within Isaiah 56–66 one sees another tendency in recent scholarship. Even while the unity of the book of Isaiah is sometimes reasserted, the disunity of Trito-Isaiah is often raised. As Joseph Blenkinsopp has summed up much of the current scholarship and debate over questions of authorship: "It will be clear by now that *chs. 56–66 do not come from one hand or from one time period.*"[8] If Blenkinsopp is correct—and I believe

[5] See Marvin Sweeney, *Isaiah 1–4 and the Post-Exilic Understanding of the Isaianic Tradition*, BZAW 171 (Berlin: De Gruyter, 1988). Summing up the findings of a number of redaction-critical studies on Isaiah, Sweeney writes: "Not only do their studies indicate that chapters 40–66 build upon themes, concepts, and language from chapters 1–39, but that the first part of the book is presented in such a way as to anticipate the concerns of the second. In other words, the two parts of the book cannot be properly understood in isolation from each other, they must be understood as two interrelated components of a redactionally unified whole" (p. 5). Odil H. Steck ("Tritojesaja im Jesajabuch," in *The Book of Isaiah / Le Livre D'Isaïe : Les Oracles Et Leurs Relectures Unité Et Complexité De L'Ouvrage*, ed. J. Vermeylen [Leuven: Leuven University Press, 1989], 361–406) also makes a compelling case that Trito-Isaiah cannot be simply separated from the book of Isaiah as a whole since each successive redaction of the former also involves a reworking of the latter.

[6] Paul Niskanen, "Yhwh as Father, Redeemer, and Potter in Isaiah 63:7–64:11," *CBQ* 68 (July 2006): 397–407.

[7] Very recently Shalom Paul (*Isaiah 40–66: Translation and Commentary* [Grand Rapids, MI: Eerdmans, 2012], 5–12) has made a strong case for authorial unity. He notes that the natural break is not between chapters 55 and 56 but between 48 and 49 as the setting shifts from Babylon to Judea. That Deutero-Isaiah may have "practiced what he preached" and returned to Jerusalem to continue his prophetic ministry is not a far-fetched hypothesis.

[8] Joseph Blenkinsopp, *Isaiah 56–66: A New Translation with Introduction and Commentary*, AB 19b (New York: Doubleday, 2003), 59. While Blenkinsopp represents the majority opinion of current scholarship, an earlier generation was equally convinced of Trito-Isaian unity. The most thorough arguments based on literary analysis were put forward by Karl Elliger (*Die Einheit des Tritojesaja* [Stuttgart: Kohlhammer, 1928]) and Hugo Odeberg (*Trito-Isaiah [Isaiah 56–66]: A Literary and Linguistic Analysis* [Uppsala:

he may be—a commentary on Isaiah 56–66 such as this one, focusing on the "final form" of the text—must exercise caution.[9] Any attempt to read Trito-Isaiah simply as one of three self-contained and unified works by three distinct authors within the book of Isaiah is doomed to failure. Adopting such an approach, one would miss both the complexities within chapters 56–66 as well as the connections between these chapters and the rest of the book of Isaiah. It is more prudent to proceed along the lines of arguing that chapters 56–66 constitute an identifiable unit within the book of Isaiah, while recognizing that other dividing lines are in fact possible. The genesis of these chapters is then beyond the scope of this commentary, but the recognition that this unit possesses a certain inner logic to be seen in rhetorical structure, vocabulary, and key themes allows for a closer examination of these elements. Whether Duhm's hypothesis concerning the divisions within Isaiah is the best way of structuring the literary treatment of the book is a question open to debate, but it is the hypothesis from which we now proceed.

As I began to write the present commentary, an interesting development presented itself in the form of computer software developed by an Israeli team headed by Moshe Koppel. The software "analyzes style and word choices to distinguish parts of a single text written by different authors."[10] As a test, it was run on the book of Isaiah, and it did indeed

---

Lundequistska, 1931]). At the same time, Charles C. Torrey (*The Second Isaiah: A New Interpretation* [New York: Charles Scribner's Sons, 1928]) was arguing for the unity of Isa 40–66.

[9] I find the argument for different time periods more compelling than that for different hands, and even on this point a word of clarification is necessary. When scholars speak of the redactional stages and "time periods" of Trito-Isaiah, these can frequently run from the end of the sixth century on into the second century BCE. This obviously necessitates the conjecture of many hands as well. I have yet to see, however, a compelling argument for some of the very late datings. All of chapters 56–66 can quite easily be understood against the backdrop of the early postexilic period (late sixth to early fifth centuries), especially in their focus on the restoration of Jerusalem. The differences in content, language, and style one encounters are certainly not beyond the range of a single author (pace Seizo Sekine, *Die Tritojesajanische Sammlung [Jes 56–66] redaktionsgeschichtlich untersucht*, BZAW 175 [Berlin: de Gruyter, 1989], 239–84; and Blenkinsopp, *Isaiah 56–66*, 59) and may reflect the author's adapted response to developments over the span of decades rather than centuries. Ultimately these questions of authorship and dating are not germane here. It simply must be pointed out that the arguments for unity in Trito-Isaiah (which is presupposed to some extent by a literary analysis of chapters 56–66) are not without their merits, but at the same time they should be taken in the broader context of the composition of the book of Isaiah.

[10] Matti Friedman, "An Israeli Algorithm Sheds Light on Distinct Writing Styles Found within Bible," *The Ledger* (June 30, 2011).

support the consensus that Isaiah is the product of more than one hand. Instead of seeing the break between First and Second Isaiah as occurring between chapters 39 and 40, however, it situated it somewhat earlier in chapter 33.[11] Also of interest is the fact that the program reported no change in authorship between chapters 55 and 56. This is yet another sober reminder that our knowledge is imperfect, and our best hypotheses of today are always subject to further analysis and revision.

Given the caveats mentioned above, it does seem right and good nevertheless to comment on Isaiah 56–66 as a cohesive unit. There is, as Paul Hanson argues, a unity of tradition if not of authorship.[12] If one goes this route, however, one must also recognize the broader unity between the variously numbered parts of the book of Isaiah and their traditions. The distinctions we then make between them are still largely driven by chronological mileposts. Thus the postexilic Judean setting provides a new historical stage within the pages of the book of Isaiah.[13] Even if these chapters themselves originate from many hands and their composition spans many decades or even centuries, there is at least this historical baseline that justifies an examination of these final chapters of the book of Isaiah as a unit. Furthermore, the new theological issues raised in this context, whether by the same or different author(s) of earlier chapters in Isaiah, warrant a focused examination of Third Isaiah's language, style, rhetoric, imagery, and, above all, theology. However one breaks down the divisions within the book, it is Third (or maybe we should say "Last") Isaiah who gives us the book of Isaiah as we know it today.

Trito-Isaiah and the Book of Isaiah

Given that Trito-Isaiah exists only as part of the larger scroll of the Prophet Isaiah, some preliminary observations on the message of

---

[11] Ibid.

[12] Paul Hanson, *The Dawn of Apocalyptic* (Philadelphia: Fortress Press, 1975), 60n29.

[13] As already noted, some would argue that there is no locational change between Second and Third Isaiah, both being written from Judea (Tiemeyer, *For the Comfort of Zion*). A temporal change is more evident and universally recognized as the context is clearly postexilic, although how far into the postexilic period continues to be debated. Jacques Vermeylen (*Du Prophète Isaïe à l'apocalyptique. Isaïe I–XXXV, miroir d'un demi-millénaire d'expérience religieuse en Isräel*, 2 vols., EBib [Paris: Gabalda, 1977–78]) argues for a first edition of Trito-Isaiah from the middle of the fifth century BCE that went through a number of redactions until its final form in the middle of the third century BCE.

Trito-Isaiah in relation to the book of Isaiah are in order.[14] These will be further developed and expanded in the commentary on particular sections. The name Isaiah means "Yhwh saves." Never was a prophet's name more apropos as a summary of his message. The book of Isaiah speaks of God's salvation and deliverance from the time of the Syro-Ephraimite War to the reconstruction of the postexilic period. Yhwh's salvation in Isaiah is, however, neither unconditional nor universal. It first of all requires and depends on a human response of right action or justice. The opening chapter of Isaiah calls on the people to:

> Wash yourselves! Clean yourselves!
>   Put away your evil deeds from before my eyes!
> Cease to do evil!
>   Learn to do good!
> Seek out justice! . . .
> If you are willing and obey,
>   you will eat the good of the land;
> but if you refuse and disobey,
>   you will be eaten by the sword;
> for the mouth of Yhwh has spoken. (Isa 1:16-17a; 19)

The contingency of the promise of well-being and salvation could hardly be more emphatically expressed. It is a conversion to just living that is the prerequisite for receiving the gift of Yhwh. The opening chapter goes on to state: "Zion shall be saved by justice, and her repentant ones by righteousness" (Isa 1:27).

Second, the salvation proclaimed in the book of Isaiah is associated with a remnant that will survive. This remnant is closely connected to the city of Jerusalem, as already evident in the previous quotation from Isaiah 1:27, which speaks of salvation for the repentant in Zion. Historically, the remnant that is daughter Zion (Isa 1:8) can be traced back to the events of the Syro-Ephraimite War (735–734 BCE) and the Assyrian invasion by the forces of Sennacherib (701 BCE) in which Jerusalem survived these onslaughts, albeit not without experiencing something of the surrounding devastation (Isa 1:7-8). Theologically, the underlying reason

---

[14] While some have argued that Trito-Isaiah at one point was an independent composition that was added to the scroll of Isaiah only after its completion as a self-standing work (e.g., Claus Westermann, *Isaiah 40–66: A Commentary*, OTL [Philadelphia: Westminster, 1969]), this position is difficult to hold today. More likely is the theory that sees Trito-Isaiah as the final redactor(s) of the book of Isaiah, responsible not only for the final eleven chapters but the reshaping of earlier material as well (Steck, "Tritojesaja im Jesajabuch"; see also Rolf Rendtorff, "Zur Komposition des Buches Jesaja," *VT* 34 [1984]: 295–320).

for Jerusalem's being the geographic location of this remnant is Yhwh's holy dwelling there on Mount Zion. This limited historical salvation for the remnant in Zion is nevertheless a symbol and a promise of something greater. A more universal state of peace and salvation is envisioned in a future time when all the nations of the world will share in Zion's blessings (Isa 2). Zion, the redeemed city in Isaiah, paradoxically stands for the redemption of a select few as well as the salvation of the many.

These pan-Isaian themes are clearly evident in the concluding chapters of the book. Trito-Isaiah takes up the vocabulary and theology of Isaiah of Jerusalem from the eighth century and applies them to his own time and circumstances. Salvation brought on by justice, the peace and welfare of Jerusalem, a remnant that is redeemed, and hints of a future universalism are all continued in Trito-Isaiah. But in recalling these great themes, Trito-Isaiah also expands on them, adding imagery that is more distinctively his own while still evoking earlier Isaian texts. Among these images, those of light, garments and adornment, building or construction, and the celebration of a wedding are especially prominent in Trito-Isaiah as symbols of salvation. The tensions in the book of Isaiah—between the remnant and the many, and between God's gifts of peace and salvation and the demand for human acts of justice—reach their climax in Trito-Isaiah.

In the drama between human and divine activity in Isaiah, Trito-Isaiah synthesizes the theology of the whole book by tightening the intricate connection between divine grace and salvation on the one hand and human works and acts of justice on the other. The link between justice (*mšpṭ*) and salvation (*yšwʿh*) is expressed most succinctly in the single word "righteousness" (*ṣdqh*), which, while prominent throughout the book of Isaiah, is uniquely used by Trito-Isaiah to express both sides of this duality—the divine gift of salvation and the human acts of justice required for its realization. One can see in the opening verse of Trito-Isaiah (Isa 56:1) this double reality expressed quite concisely in a poetic verse that could represent the main thesis of the prophet.

If the bonds that tie Isaiah 56–66 to Isaiah 1–39 are strong, those that unite these final chapters to Isaiah 40–55 are even stronger. Historically, the Isaian promise of salvation for a remnant is seen as coming to fulfillment in the return of exiles to Jerusalem throughout Isaiah 40–66. In the context of this historical moment, Yhwh is called Israel's Redeemer (an otherwise rare designation for the God of Israel) numerous times in chapters 40–66 of Isaiah.[15] The historical and theological continuity between Second and Third Isaiah finds expression in many other similarities of

---

[15] Niskanen, "Yhwh as Father," 402. The term "redeemer" (*gʾl*) is used of Yhwh thirteen times in Isa 40–66 and only five times in the rest of the Hebrew Bible.

terminology and ideas as well. Blenkinsopp lists some of the more significant themes and terms: comfort, the coming of God (with power),
the glory of God, the creator God, justice/righteousness/salvation, and
the servant/servants.[16] Seizo Sekine has given an even more extensive
list of common themes.[17] Most recently, Shalom Paul has provided both
a table of corresponding terms from Deutero- and Trito-Isaiah (or what
he calls the earlier and latter prophecies of Deutero-Isaiah) and a list of
ideas common to both sections. Among the themes common to Isaiah
40–55 and 56–66 which he notes that have not already been mentioned
are the expectation of an ingathering, daughter Zion, an eternal covenant,
female images of Yhwh, and an ambivalent attitude toward the nations.[18]

Literary Analysis of Isaiah 56–66

Since there have been numerous commentaries written on Trito-Isaiah
(including those contained within commentaries on Isa 1–66 and Isa
40–66) from a predominantly historical-critical perspective, it is not the
intention here to repeat the many arguments made concerning questions
of date, authorship, sources, formation history, historical background,
etc. Rather, the idea behind the present work is to focus on the "final
form" of chapters 56–66 as a literary composition. As I mentioned at
the outset, this literary focus does not preclude historical questions,
which are to a certain extent inextricably linked to any literary work.
What it does mean is that I intend to treat the received text(s) with all
due seriousness and keep the complex questions concerning the (in all
probability) complicated history of the text of Trito-Isaiah to the necessary minimum. If one's focus is on the formation of a text, one is free
to prefer any of several hypothetical earlier versions of a text (as commentators frequently do). But in so doing, there is the danger of being
dismissive of certain parts of the text that have been "demoted" by the
unflattering designations of interpolations, glosses, or late additions.
Such an approach fails to explain the coherence and meaning of a text as
constructed by the final editor(s) and as received by faith communities.
My intention is to attempt to address these questions of coherence and
meaning, proceeding along the following lines.

---

[16] Blenkinsopp, *Isaiah 56–66*, 31–33.
[17] Sekine, *Tritojesajanische Sammlung*, 183–216.
[18] Paul, *Isaiah 40–66*, 10–11.

First of all, I would like to pay careful attention to the vocabulary of Trito-Isaiah. The widespread use of a number of key terms throughout these chapters allows the careful reader to discern unifying thought patterns throughout the work. Texts that on the surface might appear to be disconnected or even at odds with one another can suddenly appear in a new light when considering these textual echoes and refrains that run like threads through Trito-Isaiah.

Attention to the poetry of Trito-Isaiah then expands upon this lexical analysis. The combination and arrangement of key terms in poetical parallelism helps to clarify what Trito-Isaiah understands by each word as well as showing the broader picture of a coherent theology built upon this vocabulary. To take perhaps the most significant example, the key term *ṣdqh* is alternately paired with *mšpṭ* and *yšw'h* to great effect as we shall soon see from the very opening verse. Significant word play also connects key portions of the text, such as the use of *'mmym* (Isa 56:7; 61:9; 62:10; 63:3, 6) and *'mmym* (Isa 60:2) with roughly synonymous meaning ("peoples"/"nations") at the beginning and throughout the core of Trito-Isaiah. Structuring elements such as verse patterns and chiasm both proximate and distant also help to organize the thought of Trito-Isaiah. Another prominent feature in the poetry of Trito-Isaiah is the use of triplets, or the threefold repetition of key words within a brief poetical sequence. This draws heightened attention to the significance of the idea or image thus repeated.

Within the poetry of Trito-Isaiah one also encounters a wealth of symbolic imagery. Attention will be given to the images and symbols used by Trito-Isaiah in communicating his message. Trito-Isaiah likes to mix and blend metaphorical images, often clustered under a central metaphor. Here, there are often connections between images that might not be immediately apparent to the casual modern reader. To give one example, the wedding imagery of Isaiah 62:4-5 can be seen to extend also into the images of a new name and crown (Isa 62:2-4). The imagery of crowning and adornment also flows between symbolism associated with a wedding and with military victory (Isa 61:10–62:3). In addition to these connections, there are often startling contradictions and tensions between the images used by Trito-Isaiah. Yhwh can be described in one moment as a nursing mother and in the very next as a conquering warrior (Isa 66:13-14). The varied and complex imagery that the prophet employs to speak of Yhwh and his actions reveals a sophisticated and nuanced theology of the ultimate incomparability of Yhwh.

Special care will be devoted to the study of the intratextual allusions, highlighting a certain unity to Trito-Isaiah even amid its many paradoxes. The all-too-evident tensions in the text need not lead to its fragmentation. Rather, they reveal a complex and nuanced thought beyond that of the caricatures of one-note ideologues so often constructed by scholars.[19] Here, we will attempt to read these eleven chapters together. Even if there be multiple authors and redactional layers spanning a compositional history of greater or lesser length, the parts take on a new meaning in light of their present arrangement. There are ample literary clues that these chapters did not simply accrue as a hodgepodge but are meant to be read in their present proximity within the book of Isaiah.

And finally, the connections between Trito-Isaiah and the "other Isaiahs" will be highlighted. Whether or not Trito-Isaiah ever existed as an independent composition before becoming part of the book of Isaiah is an open question. The fact is, however, that we know it only as part of this larger work. Any literary commentary on Trito-Isaiah should come to grips with how to understand this piece in its larger literary context. There are especially profound literary (and undoubtedly historical as well) ties between chapters 56–66 and chapters 40–55. Key vocabulary, imagery, and themes unite these chapters. One may note, for example, the many references to the servant(s) of Yhwh and the designation of Yhwh as Israel's redeemer (*gʾl*). And although the historical connection between Isaiah 56–66 and Isaiah 1–39 is far more remote, the literary links are unmistakable as a simple comparison of the opening and closing of the book clearly demonstrates.[20]

Themes and Theology

This literary analysis, therefore, intends to arrive ultimately at a thematic analysis of Third Isaiah's thought understood in relation to First and Second Isaiah. The theology of the book of Isaiah reaches its final synthesis in chapters 56–66. It can be argued, of course, that any attempt to extract a unified theology from these chapters, whose authorial unity is questioned and whose historical contexts are widely debated and to a large extent unknown, is a futile enterprise. It is not my intention to construct such a systematic theology from the text of Trito-Isaiah but rather to highlight running and recurring themes throughout these chapters. There are, in fact, several pronounced emphases throughout Isaiah 56–66 that merit consideration in themselves, in relation to one another, and with reference to the book of Isaiah. Many of these themes have already come up in a discussion of Trito-Isaiah in relation to the rest of the book of Isaiah. One might say this is due to the fact that the threads that tie chapters 56–66 to chapters 1–55 are to a certain extent the same

---

[19] One recalls, for example, Duhm's inaugural characterization of Trito-Isaiah as a thoroughgoing theocrat (*Das Buch Jesaja*, 418).

[20] See Sweeney, *Isaiah 1–4*.

ones that hold Trito-Isaiah together. It is worthwhile mentioning some of these here at the outset.

Yhwh Alone

Trito-Isaiah has a pronounced focus on the imminent future and Yhwh's impending action on behalf of his people. There is a strong emphasis on the transcendence and incomparability of Yhwh, who alone brings about victory and redemption. The solitary action of Yhwh in defeating his enemies (Isa 59:16-18; 63:3-5) and saving and redeeming his people (Isa 60:16; 63:8-9) emphasizes the gratuitous and miraculous nature of the present and future transformation. Yet this gracious and exclusive action of Yhwh demands a similar exclusive response on the part of the people. Those who would combine the worship of Yhwh with injustice (Isa 58:3-4; 61:8) or with the worship of other gods (Isa 65:3-4, 11) are singled out for severe judgment. There is no place for a worship that is merely formal ritual or for any type of syncretism.

The incomparability of Yhwh is, somewhat paradoxically, frequently accentuated with references to his glory (*kbwd*) and accompanying imagery of light, radiance, and splendor. While present in many passages, this luminous depiction of the coming of Yhwh is brightest in the central text of Isaiah 60, especially at its beginning (Isa 60:1-3) and its end (Isa 60:19-20). There are many other images that Trito-Isaiah employs in order to try to express the inexpressible. The language of light/glory/splendor/radiance, however, plays a preeminent role in describing Yhwh, especially with regard to his coming salvation and victory.

Righteousness/Victory

The key term *ṣdqh*, which appears twice in the opening verse of Isaiah 56–66, has a broad range of meaning that requires more than one corresponding English translation, depending on the context. The traditional translation "righteousness" refers to a human moral position and is closely linked with justice (*mšpṭ*). But the term is also used of Yhwh's action in which the "righteousness" of Yhwh is principally understood as his vindication and salvation of the righteous. In this latter sense of victory it is often paralleled with salvation (*yšwʿh*). This victory of Yhwh is also a two-edged sword, for the vindication of the righteous is inseparable from the defeat of all the unrighteous, Yhwh's enemies. One of the greatest challenges facing readers of Trito-Isaiah is what to make of the disturbing images of violent judgment scattered among the prophecies of hope and restoration. Two passages that immediately come to mind are the bloody scene in Edom (Isa 63:1-6) and the gory conclusion to the book (Isa 66:24). Far from being foreign intrusions into the main themes of Trito-Isaiah, these should be seen as integral parts and the logical extension of the prophet's thought. This brings us to the next key terms and ideas.

Servants of Yhwh and Rebels

This duality, which is found throughout Trito-Isaiah, between the righteous who will receive victory and the unrighteous who will be defeated, is reflected in the key terminology used for each group. The servants (*ᶜbdym*) of Yhwh are most likely the disciples of the "original" servant of Yhwh so prominent in Isaiah 40–55. The antithesis of these servants who tremble at Yhwh's words (Isa 66:2, 5) are the rebels (*pšᶜym*) who do not heed the word of Yhwh but go their own way (Isa 65:2). Trito-Isaiah frequently goes back and forth, addressing first one and then the other of these two camps. Thus we find a pattern in these chapters of two-sided imagery that speaks of victory and defeat, light and darkness, salvation and destruction. The contrast between these two ways runs throughout Trito-Isaiah, sometimes manifesting itself in very tight antithetical parallelism (e.g., Isa 65:13-15). In addition to the language of servants and rebels, these two groups following their two ways are also referred to as Yhwh's chosen (Isa 65:9, 15, 22) and Yhwh's enemies (Isa 59:18; 66:6, 14). The righteousness/victory of Yhwh manifests itself to each of these two groups as either salvation or destruction.

Jerusalem and the Temple

The book of Isaiah as a whole is very Zion-centric, and chapters 56–66 are no exception. Yhwh's house (Isa 56:5) and holy mountain (56:7) make a prominent appearance at the very beginning of Trito-Isaiah. The restoration and repopulating of Jerusalem are dominant themes in many of the final chapters of the book of Isaiah. Most notably we have the concluding vision in Isaiah 66 where Jerusalem, and more specifically the temple mount, is the location and instrument for the comforting of Yhwh's people, as well as the destination of peoples from all the earth who will come to see Yhwh's glory. It is from the midst of Jerusalem and the temple that the voice of Yhwh will thunder forth in the final scene of coming retribution (Isa 66:6). While some scholars have focused largely on the text of Isaiah 66:1-3 to argue for a rejection of the temple and temple sacrifice on the part of Trito-Isaiah, this argument is difficult, if not impossible, to maintain in light of the many other passages in which Yhwh's house and mountain play such key positive roles.[21] We will again want to consider the whole of chapters 56–66 in order to find a nuanced understanding of Trito-Isaiah's Zion theology. In this broader perspective, Jerusalem and the temple are of central importance to Trito-Isaiah, who can nevertheless be very critical of the practices of temple personnel. This ambivalent or nuanced attitude with respect to the temple can also be found with respect to the nations.

The Peoples and Nations in Yhwh's Plan

That Trito-Isaiah has much to say about the nations is without question. Exactly what he does say is often a matter of debate. The opening oracle speaks of the inclusion of two groups—eunuchs and foreigners—who were traditionally barred from access to the temple. Other texts, most notably in the "core" of Trito-Isaiah (Isa 60–62) and in its conclusion (Isa 66) will be more ambiguous as to the place foreigners find in Trito-Isaiah's worldview. On the one hand, these texts mention the gathering of nations in Jerusalem. They are not only included among Yhwh's people (Isa 56:3) and admitted to the temple (Isa 56:7), but Yhwh even promises to take some of them to be priests at the final gathering of nations to Jerusalem (Isa 66:21). On the other hand the role that these nations have in this new world order can in other places be seen as servile or second class (e.g., Isa 60:12, 14). What is clear is that the focus of Trito-Isaiah's message broadly includes these nations. We will have to probe deeper into the specific texts in order to weigh and judge the actual content of that message. In doing so we will want to avoid any over-simplifications that would label Trito-Isaiah as "universalistic" or "nationalistic" or "sectarian." Here, as in other instances, the thought of Trito-Isaiah is complex and nuanced. Rather than favoring certain passages over others, we shall try to look at the total picture presented by these chapters in order to discern the place of the peoples and nations in Trito-Isaiah.

---

[21] The viewpoint that sees here a radical rejection of temples and sacrifice is developed most thoroughly by Georg Fohrer, "Kritik an Tempel, Kultus und Kultusausübung in nachexilischer Zeit (Jes 56,9–57,13; 65:1-7; Hag; Mal)," in *Archäologie und Altes Testament: Festschrift f. Kurt Galling z. 8. Jan. 1970* (Tübingen: Mohr Siebeck, 1970), 101–16.

ISAIAH 56–57

Opening Oracle and Beatitude: Isaiah 56:1-2

Since there exist no independent manuscripts of Trito-Isaiah, the beginning of this portion of the book of Isaiah is itself a matter of hypothetical conjecture. My starting point has been determined for me according to the hypothesis of Duhm. Before setting out with a commentary on chapters 56–66 of Isaiah, however, it is worth noting that this hypothesis has not met with universal agreement. In addition to scholars who doubt the distinction made between Second and Third Isaiah, there are those who will accept the distinction but choose a different line of demarcation.[1] If an introduction or opening passage of an author can set the theme of an entire work (consider the effect of the stirring imperatives to comfort God's people and Jerusalem at the beginning of Deutero-Isaiah), it would seem crucial to start at the right spot. One intriguing

---

[1] Torrey (*The Second Isaiah*) gave one of the strongest reactions to the thesis of a Third Isaiah, arguing for a single author of chaps. 40–66. More recently, Christopher Seitz ("Isaiah, Book of [Third Isaiah]," in *ABD*, vol. 3, 501–7) first questioned the idea of different authorship for Isa 40–55 and 56–66 since the differences could be explained in terms of different subject matter rather than different time period. In his more recent *NIB* commentary ("The Book of Isaiah 40–66," in *NIB*, vol. 6, 309–552), he argues for a distinction to be made between chaps. 40–53 and 54–66 since in the former chapters the "servant of Yhwh" is spoken about in the singular, while the latter chapters speak of "servants" in the plural (*NIB*, 317). Ulrich Berges, in a paper delivered at the SBL in Chicago in 2012, raised the possibility of starting Trito-Isaiah with Isa 54:21b as the "title verse" of this final section. His argument is supported by three textual breaks in 1QIsa᷎ that mark a new section beginning at that point. In addition to a line break in the middle of Isa 54:17, there is an added space between lines and a *paragraphos* in the margin marking a new section. "This is the inheritance of the servants of Yhwh," which begins the new section, would then be the title or theme of Trito-Isaiah.

alternative to Duhm's choice for marking the beginning of this work within a work is the proposal of Ulrich Berges who argues on textual grounds for Isaiah 54:17b as perhaps the opening of Trito-Isaiah.[2] I find the argument rather compelling, and although I will not be offering an extended commentary on Isaiah 55 here, we may note that the opening themes of the inheritance (*nḥlt*) and the victory/righteousness (*ṣdqh*) of the servants of Yhwh give a more optimistic tone to Trito-Isaiah than is sometimes admitted when starting with chapter 56 and its mixture of hopes (Isa 56:1-8) and threats (Isa 56:9-12). Likewise, the grace and inscrutable action of Yhwh, so prominent in chapter 55, are themes that echo throughout chapters 56–66.

Suffice it here to say that Isaiah 56 does not appear as a dramatic intrusion clearly marking a new and entirely different piece of text. Rather, it continues and develops the language and thought of the preceding chapters. We begin, then, where we do as a matter of convention as much as (or more than) conviction.

Starting with chapter 56 as we are here, one also finds a fitting overture to the final chapters of this great prophetic book. Third Isaiah begins in full stride with themes that are thoroughly Isaian through and through. After the opening oracular formula ("Thus says Yhwh"), the prophet delivers the double imperative to observe and to do "justice" (*mšpṭ*) and "righteousness" (*ṣdqh*). The eighth-century passion of Isaiah of Jerusalem continues to burn in the latter chapters of this prophetic book. His concern for true religious devotion that is lived out through ethical conduct in one's daily life shines as brightly here as ever. These verses would appear to blend seamlessly with the opening chapter of Isaiah and its own appeals for justice and a restoration of righteousness (Isa 1:17, 21, 26, 27).[3] The unmistakable imprint of the spirit of Isaiah is further found in the second half of the opening verse which speaks of Yhwh's salvation (*yšwʿh*) and deliverance (*ṣdqh*) about to come. This salvation, which is entirely Yhwh's doing as an unmerited gift to his people Israel, has been a constant promise of the Prophet Isaiah, and Trito-Isaiah once more invokes its imminent arrival.

What is striking in the Hebrew text of Isaiah 56:1 (and what is invariably lost in translation) is the repetition and double meaning of the term *ṣdqh*. In the first occurrence in this verse, English translations generally translate *ṣdqh* as "righteousness" or "what is right" in a roughly synonymous parallelism with the "justice" that precedes it. In the second

---

[2] Berges, SBL paper, Chicago, 2012.

[3] There is a slight change in the vocabulary of Isa 1:21 and 26, which use *ṣdq* where Isa 56:1 has *ṣdqh*. There is an exact parallel with Isa 1:27, which uses the same two nouns in a bicolon as does Isa 56:1.

half of the verse, *ṣdqh* is usually rendered as "deliverance" or "vindication," corresponding to the "salvation" of the previous line. This gives us an ABCB pattern of three key Isaian terms, as has been pointed out by Gregory Polan.[4] He observes that the first pair—*mšpṭ* and *ṣdqh*—occurs frequently throughout Isaiah 1–39 (Isa 1:21b; 1:27; 5:7c; 5:16; 9:6d; 16:5b; 26:9b; 28:17a; 32:1a; 32:16; 33:5), while the second pair—*yšwʿh* and *ṣdqh*—is common to Isaiah 40–55 (Isa 45:8b-c; 45:21d; 46:13a; 51:5a; 51:6c; 51:8b).[5] Trito-Isaiah then ties the two together, as it were, in a synthesis of the first two main movements in the book of Isaiah. One observes in Trito-Isaiah the same kind of movement that one finds in Isaiah 1–55 whereby the exhortation language of doing and keeping *ṣdqh* and *mšpṭ* (Isa 58:2b; 58:2c; 59:4a; 59:9a; 59:14a) precedes the salvation terminology of *yšwʿh* and *ṣdqh* (Isa 59:16b; 59:17a; 61:10b; 62:1b; 63:1c).[6]

If one were to attempt to sum up the whole of Trito-Isaiah in a single word (or indeed the whole of Isaiah in light of what has been demonstrated above), that word would be *ṣdqh*, with its double sense of justice and salvation. While this would certainly be an oversimplification and an exaggeration, it could nevertheless serve a positive function by highlighting a unifying theme around which the many motifs of Trito-Isaiah might be arranged and organized. It has frequently been said that stereotypes exist because there is an element of truth in them. Like an artist's caricature that exaggerates prominent features of a subject, these generalizations might not fully or accurately portray the truth about their subject, but they can convey a significant truth nonetheless. One such lopsided depiction used to be frequently encountered in presentations of the eighth-century prophets. How many surveys and textbooks have contrasted Amos, "the prophet of God's justice," with Hosea, "the prophet of God's mercy." While certainly overstated, the comparison is not without its truth. The term *mšpṭ* occurs only four times in Amos in chapters 5 and 6 (versus twice in Hosea), but who could deny the significance of the term and the idea in Amos's thought. Similarly in Hosea, *ḥsd* appears but three times (to none in Amos), but the concept transcends the mere occurrence of the word.

Likewise, in Isaiah, *ṣdqh* (understood as both righteousness and salvation) is not only a key term but a key concept found throughout all three sections of the book. As Gregory Polan has pointed out, there is a development within the book of Isaiah as *ṣdqh* is first associated with justice and later with salvation. Joseph Blenkinsopp likewise speaks of the

---

[4] Gregory J. Polan, "Still More Signs of Unity in the Book of Isaiah: The Significance of Third Isaiah," *SBL Seminar Papers* (1997), 224–33.

[5] Ibid., 226–27.

[6] Ibid., 225–26.

"extended scope" that the term ṣdqh acquires as it expands from meaning "righteousness to the establishment of a righteous social order in the coming event of salvation."[7] This development, or extension, appears in miniature in the introductory verse of Trito-Isaiah, which presents justice (poetically paired with ṣdqh) as the precondition for God's coming salvation (also paired with ṣdqh!). Righteousness understood as justice (the imperative addressed to humans) is the precondition for righteousness understood as salvation (the deliverance coming from God).

We thus note an ambiguity in this key term as it is understood as both cause and effect. On the one hand, righteousness leads to salvation. On the other hand, righteousness and salvation are in some way identified.[8] The ambiguity, or multiple meanings, behind the term ṣdqh in Isaiah was especially highlighted by Rolf Rendtorff, who saw the deliberate combination of the two senses—righteousness and victory—in Trito-Isaiah as key to understanding the formation of the book of Isaiah.[9] Whether one accepts his conclusions regarding the formation of the book or not, the implications for reading Trito-Isaiah are inescapable. The term ṣdqh means both the righteousness and justice that lead to salvation and that very salvation or vindication itself. Translators, of course, are forced to make a choice, but readers would do well to keep both concepts in mind whenever they encounter the term in Trito-Isaiah.

What is missing from Trito-Isaiah's opening exhortation to do justice and right (when one compares it to First Isaiah) are the words of reproach and accusation and the threats of punishment. The call to justice and righteousness is linked only to the coming salvation. The people are

---

[7] Blenkinsopp, *Isaiah 56–66*, 33. Blenkinsopp goes on to point to the relative infrequency with which this expanded meaning occurs in Isa 40–55 and would assign one of these occurrences (46:12-13) to Trito-Isaiah following Hermisson's *qārôbSchicht* (Hans-Jürgen Hermission, "Einheit und Komplexität Deuterojesajas: Probleme der Redaktionsgeschichte von Jes 40–55," in *Book of Isaiah—Le Livre d' Isaie*, 287–312 [Louvain: Leuven University Press, 1989], 295). He neglects, however, the three occurrences of the root ṣdq in conjunction with yšʿ that Polan has noted in Isa 51. On the other hand, he adds mention of Isa 48:18 in which ṣdqh is linked with šlwm ("well-being"), expressing the same idea if not the same vocabulary.

[8] There may be one precedent for this in the book of Isaiah before chapter 56. In Isa 45:8 the raining down of ṣdq (here, masculine) is seen according to the symbolic imagery as the effective cause of the sprouting of salvation (yšʿ) and ṣdqh. Although in this case righteousness is not explicitly paired with justice in the first part of the verse, it may be implied in that it is seen (as in Isa 56:1) as the cause of ṣdqh as salvation. The alternative here (if the sense of ṣdq and ṣdqh is not developed or extended in this verse) would be that the causal relationship is being expressed as salvation *from heaven* giving rise to salvation *on the earth*.

[9] Rolf Rendtorff, "Isaiah 56:1 as a Key to the Formation of the Book of Isaiah," in *Canon and Theology* (Minneapolis: Fortress, 1993), 181–89.

called to act justly so that they can share in the beatitude of the just when salvation does dawn (Isa 56:2). The scarcity of condemnation in the latter parts of the book of Isaiah is most often associated with the anonymous figure of the time of the Babylonian exile whom we call Deutero-Isaiah. Although there are certainly real contrasts that one may draw between Isaiah 40–55 and Isaiah 56–66, sometimes this has been done overly simplistically, to the point where one forgets that Trito-Isaiah maintains its share of an emphasis on salvation and redemption.[10] Trito-Isaiah is truly a prophet of *ṣdqh* understood both as justice and salvation.

A New Universalism: Isaiah 56:3-8

Two classes of people typically excluded from the life of worship in the temple in Israel—eunuchs and foreigners—are now explicitly welcomed to join Yhwh's people in his house of prayer. For each group, the dual stipulations to "observe my Sabbaths" and "hold fast to my covenant" (Isa 56:4, 6) are the only requirements for acceptance within the worshiping community of a restored Israel. If one does see Isaiah 56 as the "opening passage of the third major segment of the book of Isaiah," this introit then heralds a notable theme of a more universal access to the worship of the God of Israel in his temple in Jerusalem, with Sabbath observance seen as the essential religious obligation.[11] These themes are repeated in the concluding chapter of the book, creating a thematic inclusio or "bookends" for the chapters we call Trito-Isaiah.

In light of what was mentioned regarding a possible earlier opening passage for the last part of the book of Isaiah, the thematic and linguistic links suggested between chapters 55 and 56 should perhaps also be revisited. Almost a century ago, Charles C. Torrey suggested viewing 55:1–56:8 as one unit.[12] Blenkinsopp, who does not endorse a substantial connection

[10] An example of this radical dichotomy, which sees the two senses of *ṣdqh* in opposition, and which therefore finds the thought of Isa 56:1 incompatible with Isa 40–55, may be found even in commentaries of those who argue, *grosso modo*, for the authorial unity of Isa 40–66. One such example is James D. Smart, *History and Theology in Second Isaiah: A Commentary on Isaiah 35, 40–66* (Philadelphia: Westminster, 1965). Commenting on Isa 56:1, he states, "There is nothing similar to this anywhere in chs. 40 to 55" (p. 229). He sees this text of Trito-Isaiah "moving in the direction of the later legalistic system of Judaism" in a manner that is "utterly alien" to Deutero-Isaiah (p. 229). To be fair, it should be noted that he also finds Isa 56:1-7 "alien in content" to the author of Isa 56:8–66 as well as to Deutero-Isaiah (p. 230).

[11] Blenkinsopp, *Isaiah 56–66*, 131–32.

[12] Torrey, *The Second Isaiah*, 255–57, 426–29. See also Willem Beuken, "Isa. 56.9–57.13: An Example of the Isaianic Legacy of Trito-Isaiah," in *Tradition and Reinterpretation in*

between these two chapters, nevertheless points out the linguistic link between 55:13b and 56:5b, which both speak of a lasting name that will not be cut off. As we look at Trito-Isaiah within the book of Isaiah in its present form, we can conclude that chapter 56 looks both forward (to the conclusion of the book) and backward (to the immediately preceding chapter). Without entering into the debates of textual formation, redaction, and authorship, one may simply note that the final text suggests a certain unity within chapters 56–66 as well as a further unity between these chapters and what precedes them in the Isaiah scroll.

On a thematic level, the question of Trito-Isaiah's universalism or lack thereof has sometimes been raised.[13] Here at the outset, the tone is definitely one of greater inclusion. The mention of foreigners is easily explained according to the putative setting of Trito-Isaiah in the mixed-race context of the early postexilic period (see, e.g., Ezra, Malachi). The welcome extended to foreigners to become part of the worshiping community of Israel reaches its apex perhaps in the concluding chapter of Trito-Isaiah. There we will hear of the gathering of all nations and tongues—all those who have not yet heard of Yhwh's glory—to come to worship on God's holy mountain in Jerusalem (Isa 66:18-21). But along the way to the dramatic conclusion of the book of Isaiah, there are passages that speak of God's vengeance in Edom (Isa 63:1-6) and a more subservient role for the nations vis-à-vis Israel (Isa 60:12; 61:5). How is one to reconcile these with Trito-Isaiah's so-called universalism expressed here at the beginning (and perhaps at the end) of chapters 56–66?

It would seem that a complex and nuanced relationship is being expressed. Without attempting to propose a historical setting for this text, which goes beyond the scope of this commentary, one might offer a literary comparison to the book of Judith. There we see a large-scale conflict between Israel and the nations in which the conflation of Assyrian, Babylonian, Persian, and Greek referents is portrayed as the enemy that must be opposed and indeed destroyed.[14] On the individual scale, however, the Ammonite Achior can find a place within the worshiping com-

---

Jewish and Early Christian Literature: Festschrift J. C. H. Lebram, ed. J. W. van Henten et al, 48–64 (Leiden: Brill, 1986), 50–52; and Odil H. Steck, *Studien zu Tritojesaja*, BZAW 203 (Berlin: de Gruyter, 1991), 41–42, 170–71.

[13] Joel Kaminsky and Anne Stewart, "God of All the World: Universalism and Developing Monotheism in Isaiah 40–66," *HTR* 99, no. 2 (2006): 139–63. The authors consider the universalistic and the dichotomous language of both Deutero- and Trito-Isaiah. They conclude that Trito-Isaiah shows "a greater receptivity to the inclusion of some Gentiles within the elect group" than Deutero-Isaiah (p. 162).

[14] In Jdt 1:1 Nebuchadnezzar (the Babylonian king) is called king of the Assyrians and situated in the Assyrian capital of Nineveh. His general Holofernes (Jdt 2:4) was

munity of Israel (Jdt 14:10). Here too in Isaiah 56, it is the foreigner who has attached himself to Yhwh who is addressed. Individual converts are welcomed and assured that their status will be no less than full-blooded Israelites if they but keep the Sabbath and hold fast to God's covenant.

The inclusion of eunuchs raises some interesting questions regarding how widespread a phenomenon this might have been. Once more, without attempting a historical reconstruction, we may observe that the only previous mention of eunuchs in the book of Isaiah comes in 39:7 (paralleled in 2 Kgs 20:18) when the prophet tells King Hezekiah that some of his sons will be taken away and become eunuchs in the palace of the king of Babylon. The inference might be that one could expect to find a certain number of eunuchs among the returned exiles in the early postexilic period. Literarily we might ask if there is some intrinsic connection between these two classes of people mentioned in Isaiah 56. It is not a common pairing; in fact, such a pairing does not occur at all in the biblical literature.[15] The one common denominator that Isaiah 56 picks up on is their traditional exclusion from temple worship that is now abrogated (Isa 56:3, 5, 7). Thus the caricature of Deutero-Isaiah's prophetic disinterest in cultic affairs and Trito-Isaiah's hierocratic obsession with them finds ready support in what are considered to be the opening verses of the latter.

Trouble in Paradise: Isaiah 56:9–57:13

If the distinction between Second and Third Isaiah is to be based on tone—where optimism, hope, and consolation give way to pessimism, judgment, and condemnation—perhaps Isaiah 56:9 is the place to draw the line. Here we have the first prophetic utterances of severe judgment against the depraved religious and political leaders of Israel in a style very reminiscent of the preexilic prophets.[16] In fact, this style, coupled perhaps with the lack of any clear historical referents in the text, has even led some to suggest a preexilic dating for this section of the book of Isaiah.[17] References to the prophets as "watchmen" (*ṣwrym*) and other

---

historically Persian. The desecration and rededication of the temple (Jdt 4:3) alludes to the original Hanukkah (164 BCE) in the Greek period.

[15] Foreigner and eunuch could, of course, be the same person, as in the case of Ebedmelech mentioned in Jeremiah 38:7. But there it is simply mentioned that this particular eunuch was an Ethiopian. There is no connection drawn between his status as foreigner and as eunuch in the narrative.

[16] E.g., Hos 5:1-10; Amos 6:1-7; Mic 3:1-12.

[17] Volz, *Jesaia II*, 207. See also the footnote on Isa 56:9–57:13 in the NAB. Others have gone in the opposite direction, dating it as late as the time of Antiochus IV. So, e.g.,

leaders (presumably political) as "shepherds" (*rwᶜym*) follows the usage of Ezekiel 3:17 and 34:1. The very abrupt switch from the joyful gathering of Israelite and foreigner alike into God's house (Isa 56:7-8) to the threats and accusations against Israel's watchmen and shepherds (Isa 56:9-11) is striking. The rhetorical force of this stark juxtaposition of texts may well be to serve as a warning that just as some thought to be outside of the community will be included, so too some of the very leaders of the community will find themselves cast out in judgment.

The introductory invocation in verse 9, which calls on the wild beasts to come and eat, is left hanging as the imagery is neither developed nor reiterated after this verse. Instead, the animal imagery shifts to a description of the watchmen who are likened to dumb dogs unable to bark out a warning, which is their normal function. It is likely that the wild beasts are a metaphor for Israel's enemies (see Jer 12:9) that are ready to attack the defenseless people due to the lack of vigilance and self-serving greed of its leaders.[18] It is interesting, nevertheless, that there is no mention of the "sheep" that would be the natural analogue for the people or nation in this scenario. Rather, the passage moves directly to a consideration of the watchmen as lounging, ineffective dogs. The implication may well be that these sleeping, overfed dogs will themselves become food for the more alert animals called on in verse 9—a *contrapasso* worthy of Dante himself.

The reference to shepherds in the middle of verse 11 is somewhat obscure. The MT appears to read: "And they, the shepherds, do not know how to give heed." The suggested emendation of *hwn* ("enough"; "sufficiency") for *hbyn* makes a more direct parallel between what is attributed to the dogs and the shepherds, but the proposal lacks any textual support.[19] Blenkinsopp considers the central lines of the verse a gloss, identifying the dogs with the shepherds (i.e., the leaders of the community).[20] It seems more likely, however, that dogs and shepherds are not identified here but rather that two types of leaders are being critiqued (as also in Ezekiel mentioned above). Hence the move to identify the predicates of the clauses is entirely unnecessary as each group has its own distinctive flaw. The dogs are never satisfied in their greed, and the shepherds lack the wisdom and discernment to govern and lead.

R. H. Kennett, *The Composition of the Book of Isaiah in the Light of History and Archaeology* (London: Oxford University Press, 1910), 56.

[18] Paul, *Isaiah 40–66*, 437.

[19] The emendation is suggested in the NJPS Translation, 2nd ed., comparing to Prov 30:15.

[20] Blenkinsopp, *Isaiah 56–66*, 144. He also notes the parallels to Jer 12:9-10 in which wild animals called to eat are paired with bad shepherds.

The dual accusations against political leaders and prophets is also found in Isaiah 9:14, where the elders are likened to heads and the prophets to tails. The reference to "all of them" (*klm*) in the last part of the verse strengthens the likelihood that multiple categories of people are being addressed here.

As chapter 57 begins, the accusations against the wicked leaders is contrasted and punctuated by a verse reflecting on the fate of the just in this scenario. The righteous (*hṣṣddyq*) in Isaiah 57:1 is obviously closely connected etymologically to the key theme of *ṣdqh* introduced in Isaiah 56:1. Here we have yet one more quasi-synonymous term thrown into the key word cluster of Trito-Isaiah. The righteous is paralleled poetically with "men of *ḥsd*" (which is typically and inadequately translated as "the pious" or "the devout"). Just as earlier we witnessed the pairing of *ṣdqh* with the *mšpṭ* characteristic of Amos in Isaiah 56:1, here the related term is paralleled with the *ḥsd* of Hosea. The eighth-century prophetic synthesis of Micah 6:8 lives on in Trito-Isaiah who likewise connects righteousness and justice to faithful covenant love.

Blenkinsopp, following James D. Smart, takes the singular *hṣṣddyq* of this verse to refer to an actual individual—the founding prophetic figure of the Trito-Isaianic school.[21] This would be the Servant of Isaiah 53 who was killed. Although he presents an interesting argument based on the alternation of singular and plural forms in an a-b-a pattern, it certainly seems to be the case that a simple collective understanding of the singular can just as easily be maintained here.[22] This seems more in keeping with the context of chapter 57, which contrasts the two ways of the righteous and the rebels (referred to as the *yldy pšᶜ* in Isa 57:4).

Verse 3 returns to accusations and judgment against the wicked. If the religious and political leaders (the watchmen and shepherds) bore the brunt of condemnation in Isaiah 56:9-12, the net appears to be cast more widely on the other side of the brief interlude reflecting on the fate of the righteous in Isaiah 57:1-2. Here, children are initially addressed (Isa 57:3) who, in the absence of any distinguishing identifying elements, would seem to correspond to the inhabitants of the land or of the city of Jerusalem.[23] It is noteworthy that the opening chapter of the book of

---

[21] Ibid., 150–51. Smart, *History and Theology*, 240–41.

[22] A point that Blenkinsopp (*Isaiah 56–66*, 150) himself acknowledges to a certain extent, noting the parallels in Ps 12:2 and Mic 7:2 where the singular is clearly used to express the fate of the devout understood collectively.

[23] The transition to a second-person feminine singular verb in Isa 57:6, would suggest that it is the mother of these children (i.e., the sorceress, adulteress, and harlot of 57:3) who is now addressed. The promiscuous mother taken in conjunction with her illegitimate children closely mirrors the usage in Hos 1–3 where the mother as

Isaiah begins with a similar diatribe against the city that has become a harlot (Isa 1:21) and against rebellious children (Isa 1:2-4). The roots *znh* and *pšʿ*, which were in chapter 1 associated with sins of injustice and violence, are now associated with sins of idolatry. Isaiah 57:3-13 contains some of the most colorful accusations and the harshest condemnations in all of Trito-Isaiah. Its imagery and language are reminiscent not only of Isaiah 1 but especially of Hosea and Ezekiel, who also use the motifs of adultery and licentiousness to speak about the people's idolatry.

In the vocabulary of the book of Isaiah, *pšʿ* ("rebel," "transgress") occurs throughout all three main sections as the opposite of the Isaian watchword *ṣdqh*. The opening verse of prophecy in Isaiah 1:2 mentions the children of Yhwh who have rebelled (*pšʿw*) against him. Later in Isaiah 1:27-28, *ṣdqh* as the cause of salvation (and perhaps that salvation itself) for the repentant in Zion is contrasted with the destruction of those who rebel (*pšʿym*). Here in Trito-Isaiah, the righteous of Isaiah 57:1-2 is contrasted with the rebellious of Isaiah 57:3-13. The lively and deliberately insulting language of these latter verses takes a number of swipes at the targeted audience through unflattering statements regarding their parentage. Of course, the well-known Hebrew idiom by which nature or identity is expressed through genealogy is at work here. It is interesting, nonetheless, that the opening verses use three parental metaphors ("children of a sorceress," "seed of an adulterer and a harlot") that are clearly verbal insults. The latter examples, referring to illegitimacy, will be familiar to virtually anyone, as such insulting accusations are almost universal. The former—"children of a sorceress"—is a bit more unusual. What is the significance of this more idiosyncratic insult in the context of Isaiah 57?

The root *ʿnn* in the Polel is generally translated as practicing soothsaying or divination but can be understood more literally as "to cause to appear."[24] On this basis Blenkinsopp understands the feminine noun here (*ʿnnh*) as a "female practitioner of the necromantic arts."[25] The masculine plural form of the same root had already appeared in Isaiah 2:6, adding to the many textual connections one may note between the opening chapters of Proto- and Trito-Isaiah. In that earlier passage, the *ʿnnym* are likened to the Philistines, and their presence in Jacob is equated with the embracing of foreigners and foreign customs. Perhaps the simplest hypothesis is that the sorceress (*ʿnnh*) is representative of an alien cult and

---

representing the nation and the children its inhabitants are somewhat overlapping images. The context of Trito-Isaiah (and indeed of the whole book of Isaiah) would indicate that the sinful mother more closely corresponds to the city of Jerusalem as in Ezek 16, although no explicit identification is made here.

[24] BDB, 778.

[25] Blenkinsopp, *Isaiah 56–66*, 163.

therefore symbolic of the idolatry that is so frequently associated with adultery in Hosea, Ezekiel, Jeremiah, and now here in Isaiah. Illegitimate children are, here as elsewhere, fundamentally symbolic of apostasy.

The imagery of verse 3 gives way to actual qualities that are described in verse 4. The accused are now called "children of rebelliousness" (*yldy pš^c*) and "seed of treachery" (*zr^c šqr*). As noted already, the image of rebellious children immediately evokes the opening accusation of the book of Isaiah. The nature of the rebellion and treachery then quickly unfolds in the subsequent verses, which allude to acts of idolatry in the usual locations among the trees, in the wadis, and under the clefts of rock (Isa 57:5). The libations and sacrifices (including infant sacrifice in verse 5) clearly connect to the worship of foreign deities, especially Molech who is probably mentioned in verse 9.[26] So the insulting metaphor, "offspring of an adulterer and a harlot," corresponds to the reality it represents: "rebellious children" who have turned from Yhwh to the worship of other gods. The opening accusation of these verses, "children of a sorceress," closely connects the image to the reality in that it implies both illegitimacy and alien cult.

This section concludes with one final contrast. Verse 13b returns to a consideration of the righteous: "But the one who trusts in me will inherit the land / And possess my holy mountain." This brings us back full circle to the beginning of Trito-Isaiah, where Yhwh said that he would bring to his holy mountain the eunuchs and foreigners who observe the Sabbath and keep the covenant (Isa 56:6). These are numbered among the righteous and considered Yhwh's people, while those who by birth and by law were thought to be on the inside have proven themselves by their idolatrous turning to foreign gods to be illegitimate and now excluded. The undulating motion of these two chapters corresponds to a process of judgment, separating the righteous from the rebels. In the former category are found both eunuchs and foreigners (Isa 56:1-8), the righteous departed (Isa 57:1-2), and those who even now trust in Yhwh (Isa 57:13b). While the shepherds and watchmen (Isa 56:9-12) and the apostate children who turn to other gods (Isa 57:3-13a) can await only destruction from Yhwh.

Grace and Renewal: Isaiah 57:14-21

The unusual *v^{c}mr* ("and he said") at the beginning of verse 14 clearly indicates the beginning of a new section with the use of the perfect verb

---

[26] The Masoretic text reads "the king," but there can be no doubt, considering the context, that the Canaanite deity represented by the same Hebrew consonants (*mlk*) is understood here.

rather than continuing the sequence of imperfect verbs from the preceding verse. The break is also indicated by a new paragraph on the Great Isaiah Scroll from Qumran. Although the preceding verse ends in the middle of a column, the scribe has begun a new line with verse 14. This paragraph extends through the end of the chapter. What is unusual is the presence of the conjunction if the verb is indeed a third-person perfect form of the verb "to say" as vocalized in MT and not a first-person imperfect, which might be syntactically connected to the string of imperfect verbs in verses 12 and 13. Hence the Vulgate follows the latter route and reads this as a first-person imperfect with the translation *et dicam* ("and I will say"), which is a possible reading of the consonantal text.[27] What is also unusual is the absence of a subject as the text stands in MT. It simply reads, "and he said," or "and he will say," with no clear antecedent.[28] If the implied "he" is Yhwh (which seems to be the case with the reference to "my people" at the end of the verse), this introduction to Yhwh's speech applies only to the remainder of verse 14. Verse 15a then contains a more elaborate formula that will introduce a longer discourse of Yhwh. Another possibility is that the "he" in question is the prophetic authority behind Trito-Isaiah who would be calling for action on behalf of his people. What is unclear in either case is to whom these words are being addressed. It might be the nations, the leaders of the people, or the people themselves. Some have argued that it is not any human at all that is being addressed but rather the hosts of heaven.[29] Indeed, it may be all of the above, or even all of creation if Yhwh is the one who speaks.

The theme of Isaiah 57:14—that of preparing a way for Yhwh's people—echoes loudly the call of Isaiah 40:3-4 to prepare a way for Yhwh himself.[30] The double imperative *sllw* ("build up") refers to the construction of a highway, a point that is made explicit in The Great Isaiah Scroll from Qumran (1QIsa\u1d43) with the addition of the corresponding

---

[27] The Septuagint also reads the verb as an imperfect with *kai erousin* ("and they will say"), but this is not a possible reading of the consonantal text of MT.

[28] Adding to the mystery is the fact that 1QIsa\u1d43 preserves the meaning of MT but appears to have the converted third-person masculine singular imperfect form of the verb. Of course, this depends on how one vocalizes the initial conjunction, but that the verb is taken as third person rather than first is clear from the addition of a *yod* before the root.

[29] K. Koenen, '*Ethik und Eschatologie im Tritojesajabuch*,' WMANT 62 (Neukirchen-Vluyn: Neukirchener Verlag, 1990), 53–54.

[30] Also interesting is the fact that Isa 40:6 contains yet another instance of the unusual *vĕʾāmar* found here. K. Marti (*Das Buch Jesaja* [Tübingen: Mohr Siebeck, 1990], 370) argues that the presence of this verbal form in Isa 57:14 may have been influenced by the earlier passage.

noun *hmmsllh*. This noun is also mentioned in the closely related passage of Isaiah 40:3. A question that might be raised is whether we are to understand this highway and road (*drk*) in a literal or in a metaphorical sense.[31] It appears to have a bit of both involved, as, undoubtedly, did Isaiah 40:3 to which it so clearly alludes.[32] Given that what follows speaks of Yhwh reviving the spirits of those who are lowly, it would appear that a figurative way is meant. Likewise, given what has come before concerning the evils of the sorceress's children, it would seem that there are plenty of spiritual obstacles in need of removal. The reference to Yhwh's dwelling in a high and holy place (Isa 57:15), however, can easily be understood both as transcendence high above our human ways (see Isa 55:9) and as immanence inasmuch as God's holy dwelling may be high, but the height is no more than that of Mount Zion (Isa 56:7). Therefore, a more literal path to the temple may be included in the figurative language of clearing a way for the people to come to God.

As a companion piece to Isaiah 40:3, Isaiah 57:14 also evokes the dialectic between divine grace and human response. The way for Yhwh of Deutero-Isaiah is complemented by the way for his people in Trito-Isaiah. Although this is a path that the people must walk on to approach the holy and exalted one, it is still the grace of God and the divine role in bringing about the return of God's people that is emphasized throughout the passage. In verse 15, Yhwh speaks of reviving the spirits and hearts of the lowly. The children have not responded to the accusations and punishments designed to provoke their conversion (Isa 57:16-17), yet in spite of this human failure God promises to heal them, guide them, and comfort them (Isa 57:18). The affirmation that this return of the people to Yhwh is, in fact, Yhwh's own doing is reaffirmed by repetition in the concluding phrase "I will heal them" accompanied by the oracular formula *'mr yhwh* ("says Yhwh") in Isaiah 57:19. While the clear emphasis on grace and divine activity has led some to doubt the possibility that the opening imperatives to build up the road could be addressed to a

---

[31] Walther Zimmerli ("Zur Sprache Tritojesajas" [1950], reprinted in *Gottes Offenbarung: Gesammelte Aufsätze zum Alten Testament* [Munich: Kaiser, 1963], 217–33) argued for a metaphorical understanding by which Trito-Isaiah spiritualized what had been understood as a literal way through the desert for the returning exiles in Deutero-Isaiah.

[32] While Isa 40:3 alludes to the actual movement of exiles returning from Babylon to Judea, few would argue that the new construction of a highway was necessary to achieve this transport. And since the construction there is not described as being for the people (as in Isa 57:14) but for Yhwh, the necessity of such a road is further reduced. There is clearly a spiritual or ethical interpretation to be had here also.

human audience, this is an unlikely and unnecessary assumption.[33] The
context of verses 16 and 17 especially make it very clear that the divine
call and divine activity expect a human response. The call to road construction is another variant on the prophetic language that forever calls
to conversion.

Another significant intratextual connection that ties together the
many layers of the book of Isaiah is the reference to Yhwh in verse 15 as
the one who is exalted and whose name is holy. The inaugural vision of
Isaiah 6 cannot be missed in this language. Isaiah 57:15 uses two descrip-
tive participles for Yhwh in its first line: *rm* ("the one who is high") and
nśś' ("the one who is lifted up"). These are the same two verbal adjectives
used to describe the throne of Yhwh in the vision of Isaiah 6:1. Throughout all sections of Isaiah, Yhwh is the exalted, transcendent, all-holy one,
who is incomparable and beyond the reach and even the perception of
mere mortals. The precise pairing of the terms in the formula *rm wnśś'*
occurs only in these two passages of First and Third Isaiah. It is interesting, however, that Second Isaiah also pairs the terms in their conjugated
form to describe the Servant of Yhwh who will be "raised high and lifted
up" (Isa 52:13). The exalted and majestic status that belongs to Yhwh
alone is thus also conferred upon the Servant of Yhwh.

The two roots also occur in conjunction in slightly different forms in
the book of Isaiah to refer to the proud and the arrogant. In this sense,
one finds these adjectives in their plural and definite form modifying the
cedars of Lebanon in Isaiah 2:13. Isaiah 2:11-17 is an oracle of judgment
on the haughty and, through a number of images (trees, mountains,
walls, ships), speaks of the bringing down of all that humans raise up.
The refrain that forms an inclusio around the passage is that "Yhwh
alone will be exalted [*nśgv*] on that day."[34] Trito-Isaiah reaffirms this idea
that any human attempt at exaltation will meet with a divine reckoning
that lays it low. It is rather for Yhwh to raise up and exalt the lowly as
he promises for the Servant in Isaiah 52:13–53:12. Likewise here, Yhwh
(his high and exalted status notwithstanding) dwells not only on high
but also with the lowly and the contrite. The promise in this passage is
"to revive" (*ḥyh*, Hiphil) their hearts and spirits. Thus the language of
these verses does not speak of a glorious or God-like exaltation of the
people as was accorded the Servant of Deutero-Isaiah. Rather, it is a
more modest, but also more essential, restoration to life and healing of
which the prophet speaks.

[33] See, e.g., Brevard Childs, *Isaiah*, OTL (Louisville: WJKP, 2001), 470.
[34] The root *sgv* in the *Niphal* ("to be high" or "to be set on high") closely related
in meaning to both *rm* and *nśś'* occurs frequently in First Isaiah but not beyond
chapter 33.

The other verbal link to Isaiah's vision in chapter 6 is the repetition of the adjective "holy" (*qdwš*). The description of Yhwh as the one whose name is holy and who dwells in a holy place vividly recalls the thrice-holy one of Isaiah 6:3. Given the context of Isaiah 57, where just two verses earlier Yhwh's holy mountain was mentioned, the high holy place that Yhwh inhabits in verse 15 clearly implies the temple on Mount Zion. This provides yet another allusion to the earlier vision that takes place in the temple. Isaiah 57:15 provides a microcosm of the Isaian paradox that the utterly transcendent Yhwh, the all-holy one, is at the same time close to the remnant of Israel. This immanence is realized most especially in and through the presence of Yhwh's holy temple on Mount Zion.

The back-and-forth between righteous and wicked takes one more turn to the wicked at the end of chapter 57. The emphasis in verses 14-19 has been on the return of Yhwh's people in a spirit of contrition and humility. Yhwh promises not to remain angry at their sins of greed but to restore, heal, and lead his people anew. This concluding verse is a reminder against any presumption on his people's part. The wicked will suffer a different fate. While some see in the stark contrast of this final verse signs of a later addition to the text,[35] it fits with the pattern of contrast that Trito-Isaiah employs. Indeed, it foreshadows the final contrast of the book of Isaiah with its horrific ending vision of the fate of the rebels in Isaiah 66:24. The verse is also a repetition of Isaiah 48:22 with the substitution of "my God" for "Yhwh." As commentators note, the repeated phrase in Isaiah 48:22 and 57:21 neatly divides chapters 40–66 into three roughly equal sections of nine chapters each.[36] Whether or not this is a deliberate structural marker, at the very least it can be said that literary and structural observations on Trito-Isaiah necessarily spill over into a consideration of the rest of the book of Isaiah. Similarly, the theological themes of Yhwh's holiness, grace, and presence in the temple, along with the contrasting fates of the contrite and the wicked, all belong to the larger picture of the whole of Isaiah.

---

[35] E.g., Blenkinsopp, *Isaiah 56–66*, 172.

[36] R. N. Whybray, *Isaiah 40–66*, NCBC (Grand Rapids, MI: Eerdmans, 1975), 134; Blenkinsopp, *Isaiah 56–66*, 173. Blenkinsopp traces this observation at least as far back as Duhm's commentary.

ISAIAH 58

True Fasting: Isaiah 58:1-14

It is difficult to comprehend how the caricature of Trito-Isaiah as a "theocrat" concerned solely with ritual observance in contrast to the "authentically prophetic" concerns of Deutero-Isaiah ever developed, given the text and tone of Isaiah 58.[1] The pairing of Sabbath observance with the exercise of social justice, with both characterized as true fasting, clearly demonstrates that these concerns are neither in direct opposition nor in any way incompatible. Trito-Isaiah is not religiously one-dimensional but equally concerned with the worship of Yhwh ritually, legally, and existentially. The false dichotomies and overstatements of difference between priest and prophet, post- and preexilic (whether referring to prophecy or Israelite religion), apocalyptic and prophetic, all collapse in the vision of Trito-Isaiah. Any attempt to paint a monochromatic portrait of Trito-Isaiah ultimately fails when considering chapters 56–66 in their totality. Hence the modern tendency to disassemble the text into strata that we find acceptable based on our presumptions about the limits to the range of concerns and interests that one person may hold.

It was noted above with regard to Isaiah 56:9–57:13 that some would assign that piece of Trito-Isaiah to the preexilic period based on its tone and message (even though there is no specific data that would warrant such an assignation). The same might be argued for Isaiah 58:1-14 in its description and placement of true fasting and true religion in the realm

---

[1] Such was the caricature proposed by Duhm (*Das Buch Jesaja*, 418): "He is a theocrat of the purest kind; he regards the temple, the sacrificial cult, the law, the Sabbath, etc., as the most important things." Quoted in Brooks Schramm, *The Opponents of Third Isaiah: Reconstructing the Cultic History of the Restoration* (Sheffield, UK: Sheffield Academic Press, 1995), 112.

of social justice rather than ritual observance. This is a prominent theme in all the eighth-century prophets. Undoubtedly, such a claim would have been made and sustained were it not for the fact that Trito-Isaiah mitigates this ethical monotheism with a single verse of ritual monotheism in the call for Sabbath observance in verse 13 that completes his portrait of true fasting.

While it is fair to assert that Sabbath observance rises to prominence in the postexilic period as one of the hallmarks of religious practice in Judaism, it is unfair to assert that with this rise the importance of social justice necessarily wanes. Third Isaiah has lost none of the burning zeal of First Isaiah when it comes to concern for the oppressed, the hungry, the afflicted, the homeless, and the naked. Likewise, Third Isaiah preserves the eighth-century prophet's concern for the Holy One of Israel. He does this paradoxically by calling on the people to honor the Sabbath as Yhwh's holy day. This is a paradox in the book of Isaiah inasmuch as chapters 1–55 mention the Sabbath only once, and not in a positive light. Isaiah 1:13 speaks of Yhwh's displeasure with Sabbath observance (along with sacrifices and other ritual observances mentioned in Isa 1:11-15). While it may be tempting to see this as entirely contrary to Isaiah 58:13, there is continuity within the discontinuity between Isaiah 1 and 58.

If Third Isaiah sees no conflict between ethical and ritual religion, it is by no means established that First Isaiah does. The nature of prophetic speech and the hyperbole by which it is so frequently marked call us to proceed with caution. The disdain, indifference, and hatred expressed toward ritual religion in Isaiah 1:10-15a (as also in Amos 5:21-23) must be understood in light of the bloodshed and injustice that accompany it (Isa 1:15b-17; Amos 5:24). It is the falseness, the hypocrisy, of the Sabbath observance that is condemned in Isaiah 1:13. This is actually quite consistent with Isaiah 58:13, which calls for a Sabbath observance without the greedy self-seeking that is condemned throughout the book of Isaiah. Isaiah 58 condemns the empty ritual of fasting devoid of an existential connection to a faith lived out in works of mercy and justice. This is the same dynamic expressed in Isaiah 1 with regard to sacrifices (Isa 1:11-13a) and calendric observances (Isa 1:13b-14). What is interesting is that Sabbath observance falls on the side of empty ritual in Isaiah 1:14, while it is grouped with the acts of social justice to be pursued in Isaiah 58:13.

After the opening verse of Isaiah 58 in which the prophet is exhorted to cry out and raise his voice like a shofar in order to announce to Yhwh's people their sin, the poetry of Isaiah 58 begins with a play on the root *ḥpṣ* ("delight"). In verse 2 the verbal form of the root is used twice of Yhwh's people with an irony that will become apparent. They "delight" (*yḥpṣwn*) to know Yhwh's ways and "delight" (*yḥpṣwn*) to be near God (Isa 58:2). Yet when they ask why Yhwh has not taken heed of their fasting, the divine response is quick to point out the hypocrisy in the people's claims. On their fast days it is in fact their own "delight" (*ḥpṣ*) that they seek (Isa 58:3). The conclusion of this passage will return to a consideration of the key term "delight" with a double reference in verse 13. If you turn back from doing "your delights" (*ḥpṣyk*) on Yhwh's holy day, and if you do not seek "your delight" (*ḥpṣk*) (Isa 58:13), then you will "take delight" (*ttʿnng*) in Yhwh (Isa 58:14).

The quasi-synonymous root *ʿng* is used twice in Isaiah 58:13-14 as a poetic parallel to *ḥpṣ*. In each instance it occurs in the line immediately following the use of *ḥpṣ*. It may also be noted that while the latter root is used to refer to the people's pursuit of their own desires or pleasures, the former is used with reference to Yhwh and his Sabbath. The contrast between the pursuit of human delight (*ḥpṣ*) with calling the Sabbath delight (*ʿng*) and taking delight (*ʿng*) in Yhwh reinforces the negative evaluation and ironic tone of the people's "delight" for Yhwh and his ways in verse 2. It is nothing more than a thinly masked self-seeking, which is exposed by their own complaints in verse 3 that they receive no recognition for their actions.[2]

A second inclusio that frames chapter 58 in addition to the references to delight (and the contrast between delights human and divine) is the mention of Jacob at the beginning and end of the chapter. As Blenkinsopp points out, aside from the bracketing references at the beginning and end of chapter 58 (and chapters 58–59 taken as a unit), the only other references to Jacob in Trito-Isaiah are in 60:16 and 65:9.[3] Might there be a particular significance to this triple framing of references to "the house of Jacob" (Isa 58:1), "Jacob, your father" (Isa 58:14), and "the ones turning from rebellion in Jacob" (Isa 59:20)? As noted earlier, the root for rebel/rebellion (*pšʿ*) plays a key role throughout all parts of the book of Isaiah as designating the wicked and sinful who do not embrace or receive righteousness/salvation. The tension between the rebel and the righteous, rebellion and salvation, throughout the book of Isaiah is especially highlighted in these "Jacob passages" through the call to conversion that makes possible the change from one state to the other. In these passages there is an emphasis on reversal, redemption, and inheritance.

At the beginning of this sequence, in Isaiah 58:1, the prophet declares to the house of Jacob their sin, but first of all their rebellion (*pšʿm*). The first inclusio promises the inheritance of Jacob to those who move beyond their self-seeking and take delight in Yhwh and the Sabbath

---

[2] H. G. M. Williamson, "Promises, Promises! Some Exegetical Reflections on Isaiah 58," *Word & World* 19, no. 2 (March 1, 1999): 156.

[3] Blenkinsopp, *Isaiah 56–66*, 176.

(Isa 58:14). The second inclusio promises the coming of Yhwh as redeemer to those who turn away from rebellion (*pš‹*) (Isa 59:20). We now
have two double inclusios:

Isaiah 58:1-14	Jacob / delight
Isaiah 58:1–59:20	Jacob / rebellion

Furthermore, the references to the inheritance of Jacob and Yhwh as redeemer also connect Isaiah 58:14 and Isaiah 59:20. For it is precisely the
family inheritance, their ancestral land and fortunes, that the redeemer
(*gw'l*) restores and ensures.[4] The references to Jacob, then, point to the
head of the house of Israel as the origin of their promised inheritance
vouchsafed by Yhwh. As the ambiguous character Jacob received his
inheritance through a number of reversals, so too the fortunes of his
children can turn as quickly as they return to Yhwh.

At the center of Isaiah 58 is the pivotal verse 8, which describes what
will be the results of authentic fasting that is pleasing to Yhwh. Anticipating the glorious vision of Isaiah 60, which describes the coming of
the people's vindication through images of resplendent light, Isaiah
58:8 prophesies the sudden appearance of light, healing, vindication,
and the glory of Yhwh to those who fast aright. These promises, which
are still conditional here in chapter 58, will be proclaimed as fulfilled in
chapter 60. The grammar of this passage is unusually reversed in that
the apodosis ("Then shall your light break forth . . .") precedes the
protasis ("If you banish the yoke . . .") in verse 9b. A broader view of
the surrounding text reveals, however, that there is an implied condition
already preceding the promise.

The prophet presents the details of the fast Yhwh requires in verses
6-7. The results of keeping this fast follow in Isaiah 58:8-9a, with a repetition of the description of true fasting in 9b-10a and finally a resumption
and expansion of the resultant blessings in 10b-12. The new condition
of honoring the Sabbath appears in verse 13, followed by a final list of
blessings. The overall pattern appears as follows, with three set of condi-
tions and their corresponding results:

---

[4] It is noteworthy that the other two references to Jacob in Trito-Isaiah have similar
themes connected with them. In Isa 60:16, Yhwh is also referred to as "your redeemer"
in conjunction with "the mighty one of Jacob." Likewise, Isa 65:9 speaks of Jacob's
"seed"—that is to say, his descendants as inheritors (*ywrš*) of his mountains.

	Conditions	Results
I.	*58:6-7*	*58:8-9a*
	Loose the bonds of injustice	Your light shall break forth like the dawn
	Untie the straps of the yoke	Your healing shall spring up quickly
	Let the oppressed go free	Your vindication shall go before you
	Break every yoke	The glory of Yhwh shall be your rear guard
	Share your bread with the hungry	When you call, Yhwh will answer
	Bring the homeless poor into your house	When you cry, he will say, "Here I am"
	Clothe the naked whom you see	
	Do not hide from your neighbor	
II.	*58:9b-10a*	*58:10b-12*
	Remove the yoke from your midst	Your light shall shine in darkness
	[Remove] pointing of the finger	Your gloom shall be like the noon-day
	[Remove] speaking of evil	Yhwh will guide you always
	Offer yourself (*npš*) to the hungry	He will satisfy your need (*npš*) in dry places
	Satisfy the desire (*npš*) of the afflicted	He will strengthen your bones
		You will be like a watered garden
		[You will be] like a never failing spring
		They will rebuild ancient ruins
		You will restore foundations of long ago
		You will be called repairer of the breach

	Conditions	**Results**
		[You will be called] restorer of dwelling paths
III.	*58:13*	*58:14*
	Refrain your foot from the Sabbath	You will delight in Yhwh
	[Refrain] from your pleasures on my holy day	I will make you ride upon the heights of earth
	Call the Sabbath "delight"	I will feed you the inheritance of Jacob your father
	Call Yhwh's holy day "honored"	
	Honor it and do not go your ways	
	Do not seek your pleasure or speak a word	

A couple of points worth noting here are, first of all, the overlap between the first two sets. Both conditional lists speak of oppression and injustice using the typical imagery of the yoke.[5] The second set also repeats the call to give to the hungry, although now it is no longer bread but one's very self that is offered. There are various ways to understand and translate *npš* in this context (e.g., desire, thirst, need, self). The term is immediately repeated twice in verses 10 and 11, and it is virtually impossible to meaningfully render the word the same way in English in each instance. Nevertheless, we should keep in mind the logical connections Trito-Isaiah makes through this wordplay. The acts of compassion for one's fellow human beings (e.g., feeding the hungry) are concrete expressions of the theme running throughout this chapter: i.e., seeking not one's own desires but those of Yhwh. These latter, then, are primarily acts of justice and mercy to those in need. If you satisfy their needs, not seeking your own, Yhwh will in turn satisfy yours.

A second observation is that each of the first two result lists uses the metaphor of light/glory to speak of Yhwh's reward for those who fast rightly. This is a major theme of the prophetic author, especially as we

---

[5] The reference to the yoke in Isa 58:9b has been called into question, however (Blenkinsopp, *Isaiah 56–66*, 176). A different vocalization of *mwṭh* gives "perversity" (see Ezek 9:9), which makes more sense in parallelism with the rest of 58:9b. In either case, whether by repetition or by paranomasia, Isa 58:9b recalls 58:6.

approach the center of Trito-Isaiah with its exultant poetry in chapter 60. The imagery speaks of divine revelation and manifestation. As the people now complain that Yhwh does not see or take notice, what is really being expressed is the fact that they cannot perceive Yhwh's action in their lives. The prophet assures them that they will do so, that Yhwh's presence and activity will become clear to them, once they change their way of fasting.

The second set of results also moves beyond the metaphorical to the literal and specific when it adds the restoration, repair, and rebuilding of the ruins, foundations, walls, and roads. The people's discouragement is undoubtedly tied to the failure to see concrete results in the arduous task of rebuilding (physically as well as spiritually) in the postexilic world. Yhwh promises that a spiritual renewal marked by concrete acts of justice will result in a material renewal of the desolation that must be Judah and Jerusalem.

The final two verses, which introduce a new condition (Sabbath observance), have at times been thought to be a later addition inasmuch as the Sabbath theme plays no part in the dynamic of fasting and social justice that fills the rest of the chapter.[6] As we have seen, however, there are literary markers of an inclusio in verses 58:1 and 58:14.[7] If these verses were added at a later stage of composition to verses 1-12, this was done in such a way that they function in the present text as a unit with the rest of Isaiah 58. Once again the people are called to pursue not their own desires but Yhwh's. While Sabbath observance here and the corporal works of mercy that are mentioned earlier in the chapter are indeed distinct, Trito-Isaiah nevertheless forges a certain connection. Observing both means putting aside one's self-interest. It means infringing neither on the rights of one's neighbor nor on the rights of Yhwh in our affairs.

The synthesis in Trito-Isaiah that finds no opposition but rather a unity in the injunctions to "observe justice" (Isa 56:1) and "observe the

---

[6] So, e.g., Hanson, *Dawn of Apocalyptic*, 101; Leslie Hoppe, "Isaiah 58:1-12, Fasting and Idolatry," *BTB* 13 (1983): 45. Blenkinsopp (*Isaiah 56–66*, 181) notes the general tendency to regard these verses as an addendum, adding the text-critical observation that this final segment in 1QIsa[a] has "an almost entirely blank line preceding it."

[7] Gregory Polan, *In the Ways of Justice toward Salvation: A Rhetorical Analysis of Isaiah 56–59* (New York: Peter Lang, 1986), 225. In addition to the inclusio that Polan finds between verses 1-2 and 13-14, he also notes the repetition of a number of words in verses 13-14 that occur elsewhere in Isaiah 58. This could, of course, be an attempt of a later editor to make an addition fit into the surrounding text. Focusing as we are here on the final form of the text, the inevitable conclusion is that there is, in fact, an intentional literary and theological coherence throughout the whole of Isa 58 at this final stage of textual formation.

Sabbath" (Isa 56:2) is worthy of further exploration. Modern Christian readers of Isaiah are likely to be influenced by the many New Testament texts in which a legalistic Sabbath observance is denounced in favor of acting with mercy and compassion (e.g., Matt 12:1-12; Mark 2:23-28; Luke 6:1-11; 13:10-16; 14:1-6; John 5:1-18). It would be anachronistic, however, to read this tension between Jesus and the Pharisees or between the early Christian and Jewish communities back onto the text of Trito-Isaiah. Trito-Isaiah inherits the condemnation of empty ritual observance from First Isaiah and the other great prophets of the eighth century. While it is true that First Isaiah (Isa 1:13), like Amos (Amos 5:21), had included religious gatherings on the Sabbath and other holy days among the rituals to be condemned (with their accompanying sacrifices, prayers, and hymns), the focus in Isaiah 58:13 is quite different.

Trito-Isaiah mentions none of the rituals or liturgical activities associated with the Sabbath that are mentioned in Isaiah 1:13 and Amos 5:21. Rather, he speaks simply of the Sabbath as a rest from one's own pursuits. The activity, or inactivity, that Trito-Isaiah associates with the Sabbath is precisely the exercise of justice via the abstinence from injustice that his eighth-century forerunners also called for. The opening line of Isaiah 58:13 sets the ethical tone of the Trito-Isaian Sabbath with the verb *šwb*. To "return" or "turn back" is the biblical language of conversion, turning back from evil and returning to God.[8] The peculiar phrase here—"turn back your foot from the Sabbath"—is probably best understood in light of the following line, i.e., to refrain from doing your own desires.[9] In this verse the things to be restrained or turned back on the Sabbath are one's foot, one's pleasure(s) (2x), one's ways, and speaking a word. True Sabbath observance thus complements rather than contradicts the true fasting of the previous verses. The restraint on self-seeking activity is the necessary corollary to the activation of other-seeking activity.

In the contrast drawn up between lip service and authentically lived religion, the eighth-century prophets situated certain Sabbath rituals on the side of the former. Trito-Isaiah, however, understands Sabbath observance as an expression of the latter. Here the historical context is particularly significant for the meaning of the text. Both here and in Isaiah 56:2, Sabbath observance is closely associated with not doing evil.

---

[8] 1 Kgs 8:33-35 provides a classic illustration of the double sense of *šwb* in speaking of conversion. Verse 33 uses the verb to speak of returning to God, while verse 35 uses it again to speak of turning away from sin.

[9] Many modern translations render the line as, "If you refrain from trampling the sabbath" (NRSV, NABRE, NJPS), which still leaves the metaphor to be interpreted. How does one trample the Sabbath? Blenkinsopp offers the concrete: "If you refrain from travel on the Sabbath" (*Isaiah 56–66*, 174).

While keeping the Sabbath did become one of the key cultic practices of Judaism, especially since the time of the exile, it was not simply a postexilic or diaspora replacement for preexilic and Second Temple sacrifices. Rather, the Sabbath observance, both in its origins and in its subsequent development, is rooted in the profound ethical dimension of Israelite religion.[10] Isaiah 56:2 and 58:13 continue in this tradition by understanding Sabbath observance precisely as a fasting from one's own (evil) desires. There is always perhaps the danger of reducing this fast, like the fasting from food, to a mere ritual that does not penetrate more deeply into one's life (see Amos 8:5). Trito-Isaiah, however, sees keeping the Sabbath not as a superficial ritual but as an exercise in virtue. Like fasting, it is an ascetical practice designed to lead us to lives not dominated by self-interest but rather centered in Yhwh's desires and filled with acts of mercy and compassion toward others.

---

[10] One can observe this ethical or humanitarian dimension in the various strata of the Pentateuchal laws and their rationales for keeping the Sabbath. While the Priestly source may emphasize the cultic dimension of Sabbath observance as an act of worshiping Yhwh, this is balanced by the other strands of the Pentateuch. As noted by Jeffrey Stackert ("The Sabbath of the Land in the Holiness Legislation: Combining Priestly and Non-Priestly Perspectives," *CBQ* 73, no. 2 [2011]: 239–50; here 241), "In both E (Exod 23:12) and D (Deut 5:12-15), humanitarian concerns serve as primary motivations for Sabbath adherence."

ISAIAH 59

The Power of Sin: Isaiah 59:1-8

Salvation, as we have seen, is key to the theology of the entire book of Isaiah. Chapter 59 begins by reaffirming the power of Yhwh to save. The parallel lines—"The hand of Yhwh is not too short to save / nor his ear too heavy to hear"—connect this chapter with the people's complaint in the previous. There, the people complained that Yhwh did not take heed of their fasting (Isa 58:3). The prophet responded by teaching them how to fast so that their voice might be heard on high (Isa 58:4) and God might respond to their cries (Isa 58:9), bringing light and vindication. Salvation is paralleled with Yhwh's hearing. The people's complaint that Yhwh does not hear and does not save is met with the prophetic response that there is no weakness or deficiency on Yhwh's part. Rather, it is the people's iniquities that have created a wall between them and their God, leading to Yhwh's refusal to hear them and cutting them off from salvation.

It is a tremendous thing to speak about a human power or capacity capable of overriding the divine will and power, yet this is the reality we see unfold in Isaiah 59. The causal force of human sinfulness behind the present situation of Yhwh's silence and inactivity is expressed in verse 2. Using two verbs in the Hiphil, the prophet insists that the iniquities and the sins of the people have caused the separation from God and hidden God's face. These sins of the people are highlighted in verses 3-8. Here Trito-Isaiah speaks of the universality of sin among his people in terms that are both literal and figurative. In verse 3, sins of commission and of speech are referred to through reference to hands and fingers, lips and tongue. These are then chiastically reversed, beginning with the following verse, which continues speaking of verbal sins but now gives concreteness to the false lips and treacherous tongue. The verbs $qr^{\jmath}$ and $\check{s}p\underline{t}$ denote a legal context. There is no righteousness in bringing a suit and no honesty in being judged. The abuses of a corrupt judicial system filled with false testimony and dishonest judgment are evidently a perennial problem in biblical, and indeed human, history. These sins are once again singled out here in Trito-Isaiah for condemnation.

As Trito-Isaiah completes the chiasm and returns to a consideration of sinful activities in verse 5, metaphor reigns supreme again. Hatching adders' eggs and spinning spiders' webs are not typical human sins, but the symbolism of death dealing and vain pursuits are elaborated in the ensuing lines. A certain degree of specificity as to the concrete sinful actions of the people is reached in verses 6b-7. Here we are told of acts of violence (*ḥms*) and shedding the blood of the innocent. Even so, a certain generic quality remains in these words as perhaps a stock phrase of rampant sinfulness. The same combination of terms is also found elsewhere in the prophets in Jeremiah 22:3; Ezekiel 7:23; Joel 4:19; and Habakkuk 2:8.[1] In the end, one might say that all the sins enumerated by Trito-Isaiah in these verses are the usual suspects one encounters throughout the biblical narrative. There is nothing unique to his indictment of the people's sinful words, deeds, and even thoughts (Isa 59:7b).

The accusations by the prophet against the people's sins are summed up in verse 8. The verse begins with this line: "The way of peace they do not know." It then concludes with the repetition of the three key words: way, peace, and know—"Each one who walks in that way [i.e., crooked paths] does not know peace." This is a clear echo of the end of chapter 57: "There is no peace, says my God, for the wicked" (Isa 57:21). The accusation (more clearly seen here in Isa 59:8) is also the punishment (more evident in Isa 57:21). Just as *ṣdqh* is understood both as moral requirement (righteousness) and the blessing following upon such action (vindication/salvation), so too *šlwm* expresses both the integral behavior that the people lack and the well-being they do not possess by virtue of that behavior. Trito-Isaiah demonstrates a remarkable ability to telescope action and consequence into a single term, whether it be *ṣdqh*, *šlwm*, or *mšpṭ*. It is almost as if the prophet is out to demonstrate the truth of the proverb that "virtue is its own reward."

Confession of Sin and Guilt: Isaiah 59:9-15a

Sandwiched between the two lines on not knowing peace or the way of peace is another key phrase in the indictment made by Trito-Isaiah.

---

[1] The passage from Habakkuk has the slight variation of "human blood" rather than "innocent blood" in conjunction with violence.

He remarks that "there is no justice" in their ways. This absence of justice will be repeated in various ways in the following section of Isaiah 59:9-15a. These verses, spoken in the voice of the people, continue the thought of verses 1-8, but the change in voice now makes this a self-indictment or confession of sin on the part of the people. The absence of justice (now understood as the right order that would be the result of right behavior) is mentioned in verses 9, 11, 14, and 15. Throughout this chapter we see the close pairing of the terms *mšpṭ* and *ṣdqh*, which was noted at the beginning of Trito-Isaiah in Isaiah 56:1. As was pointed out there, when paired with *mšpṭ* it is usually the first meaning of *ṣdqh* as virtuous behavior that is expressed, and when paired with *yšwʿh* it gravitates toward the second meaning of deliverance or vindication. In verse 11 we get the direct pairing of *mšpṭ* and *yšwʿh* with the former term now also understood in a salvific sense as the just order brought about by the saving action of Yhwh.

In this communal lament of the people's sin and guilt in verses 9-15a, the absence of God's justice, peace, and righteousness/vindication is understood to be the logical consequence of the people's own lack of these three virtues. The causal connection is expressed in the opening *ʿl-kn* ("therefore") of verse 9. The metaphor of light, so prominent in the central chapters of Trito-Isaiah, is once again used in verses 9-10 to describe the virtuous and salvific state in contrast to the darkness and blindness that the people now experience as a result of their sinfulness. If verses 2-8 spoke of the causative power of human sin to separate the people from God's light and salvation, the admission of guilt in verses 9-15a appears as an essential step in the process of salvation. While Yhwh has the power to save (Isa 59:1) and the people do not, the admission of guilt in these central verses of the chapter prepare the way for God's action described in the concluding third of the chapter.

Yhwh Saves: Isaiah 59:15b-20

The name Isaiah means "Yhwh saves." If ever a prophet's name was significant to the message of the prophetic book that bears his name, this is true of Isaiah. Throughout all parts of the book of Isaiah the theme of God's salvation holds a prominent place. From the deliverance of Jerusalem at the time of the Syro-Ephraimite war and the threat of Assyrian invasion recounted in First Isaiah to the liberation of the exiles from Babylonian captivity in Second Isaiah, the saving power of Yhwh has been a central concern of this prophetic book. Trito-Isaiah is no exception here. The main difference between Trito-Isaiah and the earlier parts of the book of Isaiah on this count is the generic and anonymous context for this salvation. This nonspecificity contributes to the universality of the prophet's message. It is the human story of sin and redemption. Presented with the accusations and confession of human sin in Isaiah 59:1-15a, Yhwh steps into the breach to bring justice and salvation to a people incapable of realizing these on their own.

The beginning of this final section of chapter 59 is marked by a play on words: "Yhwh saw [*wyr*ʾ] and it was evil [*wyrʿ*] in his eyes" (Isa 59:15b*a*). This evil is then explained in the last line of the verse with an echo of verse 8: "that there was no justice" (Isa 59:15b*b*). Elements from verse 15b are then repeated in verse 16: "He saw that there was no man [ʾ*yš*]" (Isa 59:16a*a*).[2] The parallel placement of "justice" and "man" in these lines reaffirms the universality of injustice on the human level, setting the stage for the divine action to be described that alone is capable of bringing about a just state of affairs or "justice" conceived of as salvation. Verse 16*ab* is an intensification of the previous line. The statement "there was not" (*ky* ʾ*yn*) is once more present in the middle of the line. This is the third consecutive line to use the predicator of nonexistence to state that something is lacking on the human scene. The initial verb changes, however, from "he saw" to "he was appalled" (*šmm*, Hithpael). Here we see a poetic crescendo as the author moves from describing Yhwh's observation to the reaction brought about by what he observes. Yhwh is astonished and dumbstruck by the utter lack of human action that would promote justice. That which is negated in these three lines undergoes a similar poetic intensification (or diminution in this case). What was lacking changes from "justice" to "a man" (i.e., there is not even one person who is just) to "an intercessor" (*pgʿ*, Hiphil Pt.). The idea now is that there is not only no justice, nor a single person who acts justly, but not even someone to urge or encourage just action in another. The utter lack and inability of any human activity or speech to positively contribute to bringing about justice is heightened.

Chapter 59 began with the claim that the hand of Yhwh is not too short to save. This motif is now taken up once more in the second half of verse 16: "His arm brought salvation for him / His righteousness sustained him." Lost in English translation is the demonstrative pronoun *hyʾ* in the final line of the verse, adding emphasis to Yhwh's *ṣdqh* as the decisive factor. One way of possibly rendering the emphasis in translation would be: "His righteousness—*that* is what sustained him." The imagery that follows in verses 18 and 19, describing Yhwh as a warrior

---

[2] As Polan (*In the Ways of Justice*, 293) points out, the repetition of the phrase "Yhwh saw" in verses 15 and 16 provides a stark contrast to the human situation of blindness in verse 10.

suiting up and punishing his enemies, holds many points of similarity with the passage to come in Isaiah 63:1-6. Such imagery is consistent with the dominant themes of Trito-Isaiah in its emphasis on salvation/vindication/judgment. What Isaiah 59 begins to highlight, and Isaiah 63:1-6 will further develop, is the understanding of salvation not merely as a deliverance from one's enemies but as a defeat of those enemies. The agonistic descriptions of salvation remind us of the bifurcated world of Trito-Isaiah that sees the righteous and the rebels in two irreconcilable camps. The threefold usage of the root *gml* in verse 18 emphasizes the payback or punishment of the enemies of Yhwh. Here is yet another example of using threefold repetition in Trito-Isaiah for heightened emphasis. The threefold retribution expressed in this verse is the divine response to the threefold absence of justice in Isaiah 59:15b-16a. The wrath that the foes of Yhwh are to receive will reach its gory climax at the end of Trito-Isaiah (Isa 66:24).

An Everlasting Prophetic Covenant: Isaiah 59:21

This brief prose passage has been described as an addition, a conclusion, an introduction, and a bridge with respect to the surrounding poetry of chapters 59 and 60.[3] The Great Isaiah Scroll from Qumran (1QIsaᵃ), dating to the first century BCE, has a space before verse 21 within the same line. It also has a line break after the verse. These data would seem to confirm the supplementary nature of the verse at the conclusion of chapter 59. A further matter of dispute, then, is just what this verse might be summarizing or supplementing. The most frequent suggestion is that it functions as an appendix to the whole of chapters 56–59.[4] Although I do not share Claus Westermann's opinion that it originally belongs at the end of Isaiah 66:20-24, I am sympathetic to his intuition that it belongs at the end of a book.[5] It does in fact have little connection to the immediate context and appears to be commenting much more on the author or the work as a whole. For this reason, I prefer to label the text neither as introduction, nor conclusion, nor bridge, but as "window" inasmuch as it gives us a glimpse through the text of Trito-Isaiah to the author and

---

[3] J. Vermeylen, *Isaïe, I–XXXV*, 2:471n1. J. Scullion, *Isaiah 40–66*, OTM 12 (Wilmington, DE: Michael Glazier, 1982), 169. Childs (*Isaiah*, 481) refers to the verse as an "interpretive epilogue" akin to Eccl 12:13 as a "summarizing commentary" of "canonical interpretation."

[4] Childs, *Isaiah*, 490. Blenkinsopp, *Isaiah 56–66*, 202.

[5] Westermann, *Isaiah 40–66*, 352.

authorial community behind it. It is a pause in the presentation of the main themes and message of the prophet to the people in order to reflect on Yhwh's message to the prophet(s) responsible for this message.

This verse combines the two ideas of covenant and prophecy. The language of spirit and words placed into the mouth are stock expressions of prophetic inspiration. Whereas some might see in the passage a reference to a universal outpouring of the prophetic spirit on future generations (such as one finds in the book of Joel), a more particular charism is actually spoken of here. Although the verse begins with a reference to Yhwh's covenant "with them,"[6] the words are directed to a singular "you" who has received Yhwh's spirit and words. This prophetic gift is then promised to remain in the mouth of "your seed and your seed's seed." This promise of a lasting covenant with future generations recalls God's promises to Noah and his family in Genesis 9:9 as well as God's promises to David in 2 Samuel 7:12 and Psalm 89:4-5. With regard to the former, it is noteworthy that the formulas in Genesis 9:9 and Isaiah 59:21 both begin with the construction "As for me" (*wʾny*).

It would seem, however, that the "seed" or "descendants" spoken of by Isaiah are not biological offspring as suggested in the Noachic and Davidic covenants but rather spiritual offspring or, to put it more precisely, prophetic disciples. This can be deduced both from the reminder here that it is Yhwh who raises up prophets through the gift of spirit and word (see Deut 18:18) and from the language of prophetic discipleship that is expressed in terms of father and children (see, e.g., Elijah/Elisha).

What we have here, then, is the signature of the prophetic author and the prophetic authorial community responsible for what we call Trito-Isaiah. This verse is not addressed by the prophet to the people but is placed in the mouth of Yhwh as addressed to the prophet and his followers on into future generations. As such, it makes sense to find it at the end (or beginning) of a major section of the work or, as Westermann suggested, at the end of the book itself. It seems likely that the verse did at some stage of textual development mark the end of Trito-Isaiah or the book of Isaiah. As it stands now, this prose pause stands apart from what precedes and follows as epilogue, prologue, or both. Cropping forth like an island in the midst of the Trito-Isaian sea, it reminds us that behind the words of these chapters there does indeed stand an anonymous prophet and the community that carried on his prophetic tradition.

It is a matter of conjecture whether the prophetic author (the singular "you" in Isa 59:21) is to be identified with the spirit-endowed prophet of either Isaiah 48:16b or Isaiah 61:1. In the case of the latter, the identifica-

---

[6] Reading with 1QIsaᵃ, Tg, and Vg. MT has the direct object marker in place of the preposition.

tion would seem almost certain. The mere proximity of the passages, standing like bookends around Isaiah 60, creates a powerful argument, as does the language of having Yhwh's spirit "upon" (ʿl) you/me. Isaiah 48:16b has slightly different language of the Lord Yhwh "and his spirit" sending (šlḥ) me. Here one may note, however, that both Isaiah 48:16b and Isaiah 61:1 (one could also add Isa 6:8) use the verb "to send" (šlḥ) in describing the prophetic commission. A case can be made that of the three prophetic commissioning passages in the latter part of the book of Isaiah, Isaiah 59:21 is chronologically last. The singular prophet who speaks in the first person in Isaiah 48:16b and Isaiah 61:1 is spoken about more obliquely in Isaiah 59:21 as Yhwh addresses him in the second person. To this is added the mention of a larger group of disciples ("them") as the partners in Yhwh's lasting covenant. The effect is very similar to what one finds at the end of John's gospel (John 21:24), sounding like a colophon written after the original prophet's death as his work is carried on by disciples.

Is Isaiah 59:21 a further witness to finding the connection between Deutero- and Trito-Isaiah on the basis of a prophetic father (the servant of Yhwh in Deutero-Isaiah) and prophetic disciples (the servants of Yhwh in Trito-Isaiah)?[7] The historical question remains in the realm of speculation, but the literary links between these three autobiographical passages in Isaiah 40–66 point to a tradition of continuity, as does the very message of Isaiah 59:21.

---

[7] 1 Sam 10:11-12 and 2 Kgs 2:12 make reference to a prophet addressed as "father" by prophetic disciples. See Joseph Blenkinsopp, "The 'Servants of the Lord' in Third Isaiah: Profile of a Pietistic Group in the Persian Epoch," *PIBA* 7 (1983): 1–23.

ISAIAH 60

Light and Salvation for Zion and through Zion: Isaiah 60:1-22

With the beginning of chapter 60, we enter into what many have described as the core of Trito-Isaiah.[1] Whether or not chapters 60–62 function diachronically as the nucleus around which Trito-Isaiah grew, we can say that they stand out in the present text as a center and high point in the concluding chapters of the book of Isaiah. As Polan has stated: "The salvific language and imagery of the Isaian corpus reaches its climax in Isaiah 60–62 through poetic description which expresses brilliance, abundance, beauty, restoration, hope and joy."[2] The Isaian theme of salvation coupled with the imagery of light explodes on the scene in the glorious vision of chapter 60. It is especially in the beginning and conclusion of this chapter that the imagery of light is used as the primary metaphor for Yhwh's salvific action in human history. Thus, verses 1-3 and 19-22 form an inclusio of the entire chapter taken as a unit.[3]

The oracles of judgment that have been building over the previous four chapters of Trito-Isaiah now give way to this stunning announcement of salvation that has come or is soon to come. The imagery in verses 1-3 that speaks of a light that has come (Isa 60:1) or will shine forth (Isa 60:2) situates the reader or the hearer of these words at the moment of transition. It is the imagery of the dawn, the transition from darkness

---

[1] Westermann (*Isaiah 40–66*, 296) has been one of the leading proponents of this now widely accepted thesis.

[2] Gregory Polan, "Zion, the Glory of the Holy One of Israel: A Literary Analysis of Isaiah 60," in *Imagery and Imagination in Biblical Literature: Essays in Honor of Aloysius Fitzgerald, F.S.C.*, ed. Aloysius Fitzgerald, Lawrence Boadt, and Mark S. Smith, chap. 4 (Washington, DC: Catholic Biblical Association of America, 2001), 50.

[3] Polan, "Zion, the Glory," 55.

to light that permeates these opening verses. Darkness, that even now covers the earth and its peoples, is giving way to a new light that breaks forth upon Yhwh's people. This moment of transition is emphasized through the use of perfect verbs in verse 1 (your light has come and the glory of Yhwh has shone) and imperfect verbs in verse 2 (Yhwh will shine and his glory will be seen).

This chapter connects not only with the preceding chapters of Trito-Isaiah but with the larger book of Isaiah as well. The dawning light of salvation recalls the imagery of Isaiah 9:1: "The people who walk in darkness have seen a great light; / On those who dwell in a land of gloom a light has dawned." The identification of this dawning light with the glory of Yhwh also hearkens back to Isaiah 40:5 and its promise that "the glory of Yhwh will appear." So in all three parts of the book of Isaiah we have the idea of salvation as the dawning of light—the sudden appearance of Yhwh's shining presence.

In response to this dawning light of Yhwh, which is the sign of a salvation and restoration that is near at hand, the city of Jerusalem itself is called to arise and shine. The addressee of the feminine-singular imperatives in verse 1 will soon be made clear as this apostrophe to Zion continues with references to "your sons" and "your daughters" who shall return (Isa 60:4, 9), the mention of physical aspects of the city such as "your walls" (Isa 60:10) and "your gates" (Isa 60:11), and finally the explicit identification with the city in verse 14.[4] The gradual unveiling of the addressee of this poem forms part of the dramatic buildup throughout this chapter. As the light of Yhwh breaks forth upon Jerusalem and the city itself begins to shine, Zion herself then becomes a light to the nations who were in darkness (Isa 60:3). The instrumentality of Jerusalem in Yhwh's more universalistic plans of salvation comes to the fore at the beginning of this chapter.

Here we see yet another key point of continuity throughout the entire book of Isaiah. The status of Jerusalem as Yhwh's holy city and its universal role in the blessing of all nations appears at the beginning of First Isaiah (Isa 2:2-4) and at the end of Trito-Isaiah (Isa 65:18-25; 66:10-13, 20).[5] The role of Zion as addressed in this passage also mirrors that of the Servant of Yhwh in Deutero-Isaiah who was called to be a light

---

[4] This is an example of delayed identification. See ibid., 66. See also Mitchell Dahood, "Hebrew Poetry," in *IDBSup*, 671–72.

[5] The question of the originality of Isa 2:2-4 versus Mic 4:1-3 is moot here. Whatever its origins, the passage plays a key role in the final text of Isaiah and participates in the overall Zion theology of the book of Isaiah. With regard to Isa 65–66, the extent to which these chapters express a truly universal perspective or not will be taken up in the commentary on them.

of nations to bring salvation to the ends of the earth (Isa 49:6). We may thus add Jerusalem/Zion to the constellation of Isaian themes prominent in this chapter, intimately connected with those of light and salvation.

The overall structure of this poetic apostrophe to Zion can be perceived working inward from the "bookends" of verses 1-3 and 19-22. As mentioned, the poem begins and ends with the theme of light. The light described in the opening verses is the dawn—light that is breaking upon the scene and beginning to make its appearance. The light that was promised in Isaiah 58:8 as the reward of true fasting—a light of healing, vindication, and the glory of Yhwh—is now coming. The concluding verses, by way of contrast, speak of the completion of this process, describing the light that is God's glory as fully manifested and eternally present.[6] This same pattern of movement from incipience to establishment can be detected in the middle portion of the poem, leading Polan to outline it in the following concentric pattern:

A^1 The Dawning Light of Salvation (vv. 1-3)
  B^1 The Movement to Zion (vv. 4-9)
    C Service to Zion (vv. 10-14)
  B^2 The Establishment of Zion (vv. 15-18)
A^2 The Everlasting Light of Salvation for Zion (vv. 19-22)[7]

The structure of chapter 60 reflects what many perceive to be the overall structure of Trito-Isaiah, concentrically built around the nucleus of chapters 60–62.[8]

The parallelism in verses 1-3 reveals a number of related terms and concepts in Trito-Isaiah. The opening verse parallels "your light" (*'wrk*) with "the glory of Yhwh" (*kbwd yhwh*). Verse 2b then speaks of Yhwh himself shining, paired here with his glory. Finally, in verse 3, "your light" is once again used, this time with "the brightness of your dawn" (*ngh zrḥk*). The key words "light," "glory," and "brightness" will be repeated in the remainder of the chapter, especially in the conclusion.[9] With

---

[6] Polan, "Zion, the Glory," 68.

[7] Ibid., 55.

[8] Etienne Charpentier (*Jeunesse du Vieux Testament* [Paris: Fayard, 1963], 79–80) was the first to propose a concentric structure for chapters 56–66 based on parallel themes and vocabulary. He has been followed by numerous scholars with various expansions and modifications of his original concept.

[9] Polan ("Zion, the Glory," 55) lists other repetitions between the opening and concluding verses (e.g., *bw'*, Yhwh, and *gwy*). Some of these, however, are widespread throughout the chapter, or one could even say throughout the Bible. It seems rather the expressions for light that hold the chapter together. In the opening eight lines, six

regard to the dawning and growth of this light throughout this chapter, one may note that a development is already taking place in verses 1-3. As the light of Yhwh begins to shine on Zion, she is also called to shine. As we move from verse 1 to verse 3, we can notice a new connotation to the term "your light." In the opening verse, "your light" is somewhat external to Zion. It is God's light that is shining on and for Jerusalem. By the time we get to verse 3, where "nations shall walk by your light," it is a light coming from Jerusalem. It is the gift of salvation she has received from Yhwh that now becomes a beacon for the nations shining forth from her. From being simply the recipient of God's salvation, Zion has now become the instrument of God's further saving light.

As we move into the central verses of chapter 60, the focus on Zion and on her transformation intensifies. Similarly, the relationship between Zion and the nations is further developed. Here we enter into one of the more complex questions with regard to Trito-Isaiah.[10] The earth and its peoples were described as being in darkness and covered with thick clouds in verse 2. Verse 3 then spoke of nations and kings walking by the light and brightness of Zion. Verses 4-9 now describe this movement from the far reaches of the earth toward Jerusalem. As we have seen, this is a movement that echoes a pattern begun back in Isaiah 2:2-4. The fundamental question is whether Trito-Isaiah here is envisioning a future salvation for the nations gathered in Zion or rather a reversal of fortunes in which the nations who ruled and exiled the children of Zion are now themselves brought low and reduced to subservient status.

When comparing the migrations of the nations to Zion found in Isaiah 2 and Isaiah 60, the obvious difference to note is that in First Isaiah the nations are coming on behalf of themselves whereas in Third Isaiah they are coming for the sake of the exiled inhabitants of Jerusalem and of the city itself. It is their function to bring back the sons and daughters of Zion (Isa 60:4, 9) and to bring the wealth of the nations with them (Isa 60:5-7, 9). In fact, it is almost as if these goods coming via camel, ship, and even cloud do so of their own accord, since no mention is made of foreign peoples or nations in these verses. When the peoples and nations are mentioned beginning in verse 10, it is their job to work in the reconstruction of Zion (Isa 60:10), to serve Zion (Isa 60:12), to prostrate themselves before her (Isa 60:14), and to nourish her (Isa 60:16).

---

have light terminology, and the other two have contrasting darkness terminology. Likewise, in the conclusion, *'wr* and *ngh* will be repeated. And although *kbwd yhwh* will not, its established parallel from verse 2 (Yhwh) will be equated twice with light.

[10] For the nations in relation to Zion, see James Muilenburg, "The Book of Isaiah, Chapters 40–66," in *Interpreter's Bible* 5 (Nashville: Abingdon Press, 1956), 703; Westermann, *Isaiah 40–66*, 360; Childs, *Isaiah*, 495–98; Blenkinsopp, *Isaiah 56–66*, 313–14.

The particularly negative language of verse 12 has frequently been dismissed as a later gloss by commentators, either due to its more prosaic style or due to its narrowly nationalistic theology, or both.[11] But since the dismissal of the verse does not resolve the tensions in Trito-Isaiah regarding judgment or salvation for the nations, and since we must come to grips with its inclusion in the final form of the text, we must consider it together with the surrounding verses within the structure of chapter 60 as well as within the context of Trito-Isaiah. One important connection to make is the relationship between chapter 60 and what precedes it. We have already noted the oracles of judgment (Isa 56:9-12; 57:3-13a; 58:1-5; 59:1-15) leading up to this prophecy of salvation. Likewise, the promise of light (Isa 58:8) now finds its fulfillment. Another key element in Trito-Isaiah that bears upon these verses is the contrast we have seen in alternating passages between the righteous and the rebels. As Brevard Childs has noted, this is the true polarity one finds throughout Trito-Isaiah, not one of universalism versus nationalism.[12]

In typical prophetic fashion, only one side of a conditional is expressed in verse 12: "For the nation or the kingdom that does not serve you shall perish." But this is clearly not a blanket statement of condemnation upon the nations. The implication is that the nation that does serve Zion shall be saved. This is a direct echo of the opening verses of Trito-Isaiah in which we were told that foreigners who join themselves to Yhwh, minister to him, love the name of Yhwh, and become his servants (Isa 56:6) will be brought to Yhwh's holy mountain and rejoice in his house (Isa 56:7). Throughout Second and Third Isaiah, to be called to be a servant or servants of Yhwh is the noblest of vocations. Modern sensibilities might find the substitution of Zion for Yhwh as the recipient of service troubling, but this is simply a reflection of Israel's and Zion's own servant status as a light to the nations (Isa 49:6; 60:3) as well as the special place Zion and its temple hold in Isaian theology as the locus of God's glory. To serve Zion is to serve Yhwh, which is in itself a blessing. In answer to the question "Is Trito-Isaiah nationalistic or universalistic?" I would argue that the answer has to be "Yes!" The prophet proclaims a

---

[11] Paul Volz (*Jesaja II, Zweite Hälfte: Kapitel 40–66* [Leipzig: Deichert, 1932]), who was particularly critical of the nationalism of Trito-Isaiah, considered the verse a gloss. More recently, Blenkinsopp (*Isaiah 56–66*, 215) also judged it a prose gloss, comparing it to similar judgment glosses in Isa 2:6-22 and Jer 10:11. Childs (*Isaiah*, 497) argues that a better exegetical approach is to try to discern how it functions in the chapter. Polan ("Zion, the Glory," 64–66) does precisely this, making a cogent case for the centrality of the verse in chapter 60.

[12] Childs, *Isaiah*, 498.

salvation that is open to all, including foreigner and eunuch, but it comes precisely through Yhwh's holy city and temple: through Zion.

Beginning with verse 14, the poem in Isaiah 60 contains a number of namings of Jerusalem and her constitutive elements, each of which expresses a reversal so characteristic of Trito-Isaiah's thought. These namings are also closely tied to a second round of namings that will take place on the other side of the "center" of Trito-Isaiah. Chapter 62 will constitute a second apostrophe to Zion with numerous connections to the present chapter. Looking beyond Trito-Isaiah at the entire book of Isaiah, the renamings of Jerusalem in these chapters can also be seen as the fulfillment of the prophecy in Isaiah 1:26b: "After that you shall be called the City of Righteousness, Faithful City." Isaiah 60:14b announces, "They shall call you 'City of Yhwh' / 'Zion of the Holy One of Israel.'" The close connection between Yhwh and the city of Jerusalem is expressed in these titles. More precisely, the titles refer to Yhwh's ownership of Zion; she belongs to him. In the cultural context of ancient Israel, this can also be understood as a marital relationship. This imagery will become much more apparent in the corresponding passages in Isaiah 62, but it is already present here.

Following these new names given in verse 14, a contrast is drawn between this new status of the city and her previous condition in verse 15: "Instead of your being abandoned / and hated with no one passing by, / I will make you the pride of the ages, / a joy from age to age." The use of the verbs *ᶜzb* ("abandon") and *śnʾ* ("hate") suggests a marital context in which a husband has left his wife. In fact, the verb *śnʾ* is a technical term for divorce or repudiation of a wife (see, e.g., Judg 15:2). Even the verb *ᶜbr* ("pass by/through/over") has some unexpected marital connotations that can be seen in comparing this passage to Ezekiel 16, in which *ᶜbr* is used in close connection with betrothal/marriage (Ezek 16:8) and sexual activity (Ezek 16:15, 25). From the status of abandoned and repudiated wife, whom no one approaches with marital intent, the renamed Zion will become "pride" (*gʾwn*). This term is also used in the marital metaphor of Ezekiel 16 of the proud and haughty wife and mother Jerusalem who looks down upon her sister Sodom (Ezek 16:56). In a more positive context, pride is used in conjunction with splendor (*tpʾrt*) in Isaiah 4:2 as coming upon the remnant in Zion. There it is not associated with marriage but is part of a larger cluster of radiant imagery connecting Isaiah 60 and Isaiah 4. Both speak of a reversal of fortunes and salvation for Jerusalem/Zion. And both do so drawing heavily on imagery of exalted radiance. Three key words from Isaiah 4:2 reappear in the poem of chapter 60: "glory" (*kbwd*), "pride" (*gʾwn*), and "splendor" (*tpʾrt*). Finally, in Isaiah 60:15, Jerusalem's new status is marked by joy (*mśwś*). The verb (*śwś*) will be used again with marital imagery of a gloriously adorned bride and bridegroom in the following chapter (Isa 61:10). The language of Isaiah 60:15, then, is reflective of the changed status of Zion as she has gone from being divorced and abandoned to being united/married to Yhwh.

Verses 17 and 18 contain a series of rapid-fire reversals that highlight the new, exalted status of Zion. The materials of the city undergo a dramatic upgrade as all that is base is replaced with something of greater value and strength. The replacement of copper with gold, iron with silver, and so on emphasizes that the new names for Zion correspond to a new reality. It is an actual transformation that will take place, not merely attributing to Jerusalem empty titles and meaningless words. The process of renaming then extends to the physical structures of the city—her walls and her gates. Zion shall call her walls by the preeminently Isaian term "Salvation" (*yšwʿh*) and her gates "Praise" (*thllh*). The latter term has not been featured quite as prominently as the former throughout Isaiah and Trito-Isaiah, but there is a close connection to be made here in chapter 60. The first half of the poem saw the movement of the nations toward Zion, bringing with them the children of the exile and riches with which Zion might be restored. At the end of verse 6 it was said that the caravans coming from the south, bearing gold and frankincense to Zion, "shall proclaim the praise of Yhwh" (Isa 60:6).[13] Thus the praise associated with the movement toward Zion is fittingly given as a name to her gates through which the pilgrims pass.

We may also note, in association with the theme of naming, that symbolic names of officials are given as well in Isaiah 60:17. Although these are not described as namings or renamings, the placing of these symbolic names in positions of authority within the city is closely tied to the symbolic naming of walls and gates in the following verse. As Blenkinsopp (following Ibn Ezra) has pointed out, the types of officials named (especially *ngśym*, "taskmasters") carry negative connotations.[14] The contrast, then, between the oppressive-sounding official titles and the names denoting well-being and salvation of those Yhwh appoints to these offices (*šlwm* and *ṣdqh*) gives us yet another example of the many reversals of Trito-Isaiah. While many translations understand the roles involved rather generically (e.g., "governor," "ruler," "officials"), it may be the case, given the context (and the technical usage of *ngś* elsewhere,

---

[13] Although MT points the noun in construct as a plural (*tĕhillōt yhwh*), the defective consonantal text (*thlt* rather than the usual plene spelling of the plural *thlwt*) make this more likely a singular. Thus the "praise of Yhwh," which the nations proclaim as they travel into Jerusalem and pass through her gates, corresponds to the new name given to those gates in Isa 60:18.

[14] Blenkinsopp, *Isaiah 56–66*, 216.

such as Exod 5:6 and Isa 9:3), that the prophet has in mind those charged with overseeing the labor force in the reconstruction of Jerusalem.

The conclusion of Isaiah 60 (Isa 60:19-22) features a return to the brilliant imagery of light with which the chapter began. In a verse that will be echoed in the New Testament book of Revelation, it is Yhwh himself who will be the city's light forever; she will have no more need of sun by day or moon by night (Isa 60:19; Rev 21:23; 22:5). The dawning light of the opening verses has reached fulfillment. The transformations, reversals, and renamings are now completed. The definitive and everlasting quality of this new state is emphasized throughout. The threefold repetition of the word ʿwlm ("forever") and the double usage of lʾ ʿwd ("no longer") in these verses dramatize the irreversible and eschatological scope of this prophecy.[15] We are reminded, however, at the very end of the chapter that this is a prophecy of a transformation yet to come. We have but begun to see the dawning of this glorious light in what Yhwh is now doing for Zion. Yet this work is still in its infancy. Yhwh has planted a shoot in Zion and has promised its continued growth, and a prodigious growth at that. But the future fulfillment of this vision of splendor and salvation still depends on Yhwh's action in due time. The doubly emphatic ʾny yhwh ("I, Yhwh") preceding the final verb dramatically concludes the point: it is Yhwh, and no other, who will do this.

---

[15] If one extends the analysis back into verse 18, one notes that there is, in fact, a triple use of lōʾ ʿôd as well, forming a nice parallel structure with the threefold ʿôlām.

ISAIAH 61

Yhwh's Anointed Messenger: Isaiah 61:1-11

The voice that we hear coming from the text suddenly changes at the beginning of chapter 61. In Isaiah 61:1-3, it is no longer the voice of Yhwh speaking through the prophet, addressing Zion. The first-person-singular voice is not "I, Yhwh," which we saw at the end of chapter 60. Rather, it is the individual prophetic voice speaking of itself as anointed and commissioned by Yhwh to proclaim a message to the mourners in Zion. The autobiographical nature of these verses is such that the first-person "me" of Isaiah 61:1 may be identified as the second-person "you" addressed by the voice of Yhwh in Isaiah 59:21. At the center of Trito-Isaiah we thus find a powerful claim to divine authority and inspiration. The threefold repetition of "me" in the opening three lines of this chapter identifies the prophetic author as (1) one possessing Yhwh's spirit, (2) one who has been anointed, and (3) one who has been sent. The first point in particular repeats the claim of Isaiah 59:21 (and perhaps also Isa 48:16b) that the prophet has received Yhwh's spirit. The second point has not been previously mentioned in any of the "autobiographical" passages of Deutero- or Trito-Isaiah, although there was a reference in Isaiah 45:1 to Cyrus as Yhwh's anointed.[1] The third point, while not mentioned in Isaiah 59:21, was also stated in the Deutero-Isaian signature of Isaiah

---

[1] Some have claimed that the reference to being anointed points to a royal figure in David's line (Marvin Sweeney, "The Reconceptualization of the Davidic Covenant in Isaiah," in *Studies in the Book of Isaiah: Festschrift Willem A. M. Beuken*, ed. J. Van Ruiten and M. Vervenne [Leuven: Leuven University Press, 1997], 55–56) or a priest (Pierre Grelot, "Sur Isaïe LXI: La première consécration d'un grand-prêtre," *RB* 97 [1990]: 414–31), inasmuch as biblical language of anointing is primarily used of kings (e.g., 1 Sam 10:1) and priests (Lev 4:3, 5). It should be noted, however, that anointing

48:16b. Isaiah 61:1, then, provides the most comprehensive statement of prophetic commissioning in the latter half of the book of Isaiah.

As we continue on in Isaiah 61:1b-3 to see precisely what this commission entails, we encounter a somewhat unusual turn of mood as well as of voice when compared with chapter 60. Having just concluded the gloriously triumphant poem of Isaiah 60, in which Zion is described as filled with the eternal light and splendor of Yhwh himself, how is it that the prophet still has a mission to the poor and afflicted, to those who are still captive and in prison? These two changes in voice and mood actually go together. Isaiah 61:1-3, like Isaiah 59:21, appears as a pause or a window in the text. Our gaze is momentarily drawn away from Zion and her children as the object of the prophet's oracles and shifts its focus onto the spirit-endowed prophetic figure. With this shift, we are once again made aware of the present situation in which the prophet speaks, and we realize that the future transformation of Zion described in the surrounding verses has not yet come to fulfillment. The reversals and transformation of Zion, found in Isaiah 60, are then resumed beginning with Isaiah 61:3. The mourners of Zion will receive "a turban instead of ashes, festive oil instead of mourning, a garment of praise instead of a drooping spirit" (Isa 61:3).

Before returning to the promise of a restored future, however, it is worth reflecting on Trito-Isaiah's language used to describe those whom he addresses in the moment. In addition to being called "mourners" (Isa 61:2-3), they are called "captives" and "prisoners" (Isa 61:1) although it would seem they are, in fact, in Zion now and no longer in Babylon. It appears that Trito-Isaiah is spiritualizing or allegorizing the exile.[2] The fact that the eschatological hopes and dreams expressed in the core of Trito-Isaiah are not yet realized leads to an identification of this state as being continuous with that of exile. This is akin to the book of Daniel's reinterpretation of Jeremiah (Dan 9:2, 24) by which the "literal" understanding of exile as a lifetime (seventy years) in Babylon is allegori-

---

can also refer to prophets (e.g., 1 Kgs 19:16) and that the verb "anoint" can be used metaphorically as well as literally (Blenkinsopp, *Isaiah 56–66*, 220).

[2] Bradley Gregory ("The Postexilic Exile in Third Isaiah: Isaiah 61:1-3 in Light of Second Temple Hermeneutics," *JBL* 126, no. 3 (2007): 475–96) refers to this as the "theologization" of the exile. This perspective, which sees a state of exile persisting after 538 BCE, is widespread in the Second Temple period (e.g., Dan 9; 1 Enoch; Testament of Levi 16-17; Assumption of Moses 3; Jubilees 1:7-18; Tobit 13-14; CD 1:5-11). See James VanderKam, "Exile in Jewish Apocalyptic Literature," in *Exile: Old Testament, Jewish, and Christian Conceptions*, ed. James M. Scott, JSJSup 56 (Leiden: Brill, 1997), 94–104; and Michael Knibb, "The Exile in the Literature of the Intertestamental Period," *HeyJ* 17 (1976): 253–72.

cally stretched to seventy weeks (of years) in order to encompass the tribulations of postexilic Judea as well. Trito-Isaiah's mission is to these postexilic "exiles," and his message is that their lot too shall be changed from mourning into joy.

Part of this transformation involves a role reversal between Israel and the nations. Continuing the theme of foreign service to Zion from the previous chapter, Isaiah 61:5 assigns to foreigners the roles of shepherding the flocks and working the fields and vineyards. A contrast is then made in the following verse, beginning with a disjunctive *vav*: "But you . . ." The new and distinctive role of those addressed by the prophet is once again expressed through naming language: "You shall be called priests of Yhwh / Ministers of our God you shall be called" (Isa 61:6a). The assigning of the meaner manual tasks to foreigners serves the purpose of freeing the children of Zion for a loftier role and title. The theme of profiting from the nations continues in the second half of the verse. This raises again the question of Trito-Isaiah's universalism or lack thereof. The nations find a place in Zion, but it appears to be one of second-class status when compared to the children of Zion. They render service to Zion and her children so that the latter may render service to Yhwh.

The themes of rebuilding in verse 4 and the wealth of the nations in verse 6 echo the previous chapter (Isa 60:5-7 and 10). Each of these is closely connected with the foreigners who either do the work of construction or transport the wealth. The subject of the rebuilding in Isaiah 61:4, however, is not specified as it was in the previous chapter. The third-person plural could refer to the foreigners who are made explicit in the following verse, thus reflecting the same understanding as in Isaiah 60:10. The immediate antecedent, however, is "the mourners of Zion" (Isa 61:3) who will be called "the oaks of righteousness" (Isa 61:4). This seems more likely, revealing a pattern of address in which the prophet shifts from speaking of the people in the third person (Isa 61:1-4) to the second person (Isa 61:6) and back to the third (Isa 61:7). If this is the case, then it would seem that the Israelites share in the manual labor of the foreigners. The division of labor in this case is not between menial work for foreigners and spiritual service for Israelites but rather rural service by foreigners which enables the Israelites to go about the task of urban rebuilding. Perhaps all of these tasks—rebuilding ruins, shepherding flocks, and farming land—should be viewed in a positive light, reflecting a restored urban and rural landscape.[3] Seen in this way, the nations

---

[3] One might contrast passages in which a more onerous labor is clearly implied, such as the Gibeonites' tasks of being "hewers of wood and drawers of water" (Josh 9:27).

are not relegated to second-class status but share in the common work of restoring the neglected lands and cities of Judea.

With Isaiah 61:8 it is the voice of Yhwh that interrupts, so to speak, the prophet's monologue. The intrusion, however, may be only apparent since the voice of the prophet is in fact the voice of Yhwh.[4] The prophet, who has been addressing the people in both the third and second person in the preceding verses, now shifts from speaking about God in the third person (Isa 61:1, 2, 3, 6) to speaking with the *vox Dei* in the first person. Such transitions between first and third person with reference to Yhwh are frequent in these central chapters of Trito-Isaiah. The particle *ky* ("for") with which verse 8 begins connects this verse logically with the previous verses and so should be translated.[5] The reversals and real-lotment of wealth described in Isaiah 61:1-7 are expressions of Yhwh's justice. After stating Yhwh's love for justice, verse 8 goes on to say, "I hate robbery with a burnt offering." While this sentiment of Yhwh's distaste for the combination of immoral actions and ritual religion is a commonplace throughout the prophets, including the book of Isaiah (e.g. Isa 1:11-17), the consonantal text (*bʿwlh*) may also be read "with wickedness."[6] Given the emphasis on distributive justice, especially in verses 7-8, the latter reading is certainly plausible. Yhwh also promises to give them their reward "in truth" or "with fidelity" (*bʾmt*), which directly contrasts "with wickedness" (Isa 61:8). Of the two equally possible readings here, commentators have tended to gravitate toward reading "with wickedness" by arguing for a better fit in the context.[7]

---

[4] Blenkinsopp (*Isaiah 56–66*, 228) mentions the immediately preceding Isa 61:1-3b as the only instance where the prophet speaks in his own name. He also gives two examples where Yhwh is clearly identified as the speaker (here in 61:8-9 and in 62:8) as indicative of a division in the text. While I agree with Blenkinsopp that the "going back and forth between third and first person" in Isa 60–62 with reference to Yhwh does not necessarily mark a division, I would be even more cautious regarding Isa 61:8-9 and 62:8. These could serve as emphatic reminders that the prophetic "I" is the divine "I" and need not be indicative of a new section.

[5] The particle can be understood either demonstratively ("surely," "indeed") or causatively ("for," "because"). Given that there is a clear causal connection between what is described in verses 1-7 and the motive of the agent (Yhwh) who accomplishes them, the latter is preferable here.

[6] The alternate reading is supported by LXX (*ex adikias*), Tg (*wěʾānsāʾ*), and a few Hebrew manuscripts pointed *běʿavlâ*. It may also be that even keeping the predominant pointing found in MT (*běʿôlâ*), this may be read as a variant of *ʿavlâ*. (See Blenkinsopp, *Isaiah 56–66*, 228, who cites Ps 58:3 and 64:7 as examples; also, Paul, *Isaiah 40–66*, 546, who cites Job 5:16 as well as the Psalms).

[7] See, e.g., John D. W. Watts, *Isaiah 34–66*, rev. ed., Word Biblical Commentary 25 (Nashville: Thomas Nelson, 2005), 871. Also, Paul Hanson translates "with burnt of-

We should not, however, discount the predominant reading in the majority of manuscripts in the Masoretic tradition. As already noted, the reading "I hate robbery with a burnt offering" resonates very much with an inaugural Isaian theme in Isaiah 1:11-17 that expresses hatred of sacrifices without goodness and justice. This reading can also help us make sense of the final chapter of Isaiah, where we will encounter yet another judgment against sacrifices gone wrong (Isa 66:3-4). It is likely that there, as here, it is not sacrifice per se that is being condemned but the deadly combination of cultic ritual and evil actions. At the very least, we should admit that this ambiguous text of Isaiah 61:8 is ambiguous, and perhaps deliberately so. There is a pun in the word *b\'wlh* and it is certainly possible that Trito-Isaiah wants to play on words here and to have us hear both "burnt offering" and "wickedness."

Coming to the end of the verse, Isaiah 61:8b is one of the three Isaian passages (the sole representative from chaps. 56–66) that speaks of Yhwh's everlasting covenant. The nearest antecedent in Isaiah 55:3 deserves special consideration in examining what Trito-Isaiah intends by this lasting covenant.[8] We have already noted the close connection between Isaiah 55 and chapters 56–66 inasmuch as some would consider it the actual beginning of Trito-Isaiah with the superscription of Isaiah 54:17b. Isaiah 55:3 introduces the theme of a lasting covenant, which is identified as God's covenant with David. This immediately focuses attention away from other "candidate covenants," such as the one with Noah, which is also designated as a *bryt \'wlm* (Gen 9:16). Looking ahead, this will also establish a connection between this promise of a lasting covenant and the psalm-like passage beginning in Isaiah 63:7, whose opening verse recalls the similar Psalm 89 in its telling of the promises of Yhwh in his covenant with David.

Reference to Yhwh's lasting covenant with David in an early post-exilic setting evokes Yhwh's promise to David of an enduring dynasty. While the promise seemed to fail with the exile of Jehoiachin in 598 BCE, the return from exile once again sparked hopes of fulfillment in the person of the Davidic heir Zerubbabel (see Zech 4). Isaiah 61, however, makes no references either to an individual or to a monarchical dynasty.

---

fering" in his earlier work (*Dawn of Apocalyptic*, 52) but as "wrongdoing" in his later commentary (*Isaiah 40–66*, Interpretation [Louisville: John Knox Press, 1995], 225).

[8] The first occurrence of this terminology in the book of Isaiah is found in Isa 24:5, which refers to the breaking of this covenant by the people. The close connection between the breaking of the covenant and the curse upon the earth in Isa 24:6 probably means that the covenant with Noah (see Gen 9) rather than the covenant with David is the principal point of reference in that passage. It is also possible, however, that the references to the breaking of teachings and laws in Isa 24:5 may allude to Sinai.

The covenant is with the plural "them" who may be identified with the people whom the prophet earlier addresses as "priests of Yhwh" and "servants of our God" (Isa 61:6). It should also be noted that the peculiar verse Isaiah 59:21 also began with Yhwh speaking of a "covenant with them." In that case we saw how the plural "them" was understood as the prophetic disciples of the individual prophet addressed as "you." We have also noted the close connection between that spirit-endowed prophet and the speaker of Isaiah 61:1-7. If the Davidic covenant is the starting point (beginning with Isa 55:3) for Trito-Isaiah's reflections on this lasting covenant, it does not end with David or his line but is broadened to some extent to include all the "servants" of Yhwh who also participate in the roles of priest (Isa 61:6) and prophet (Isa 59:21).

We must also keep in mind that for Trito-Isaiah Jerusalem is not so much the city of the house of David as it is the city of Yhwh and his temple. So while there is great interest throughout Trito-Isaiah in rebuilding and repopulating the city, there is no mention whatsoever of reconstituting its ancient ruling dynasty. Even back in Isaiah 55:3, where the Davidic covenant was expressly recalled, the blessing and promise of that covenant was defined as the faithful love promised to David (*ḥsdy dwd*), not as the house or lasting dynasty. This promise is seen as applying more broadly to the people in Isaiah 55:3 ("for you" [pl], *lkm*) as it also is in Isaiah 61:8 ("for them") and Isaiah 63:7 ("for all that Yhwh has done for us").

There is yet another key allusion to Yhwh's covenant with David in Isaiah 61, in which we see a further expansion of the original, literal sense of that covenant. This is the reference in verse 9 to "the seed Yhwh has blessed." The promise of "seed" (*zrʿ*) was a key component of the Davidic covenant (2 Sam 7:12). What was understood as only David's offspring, or the royal dynasty, in the initial account of Yhwh's lasting covenant with David is here taken by Trito-Isaiah as applying to the people in general.[9] The mourners in Zion, the restored and exalted remnant, will be recognized by all nations as this seed blessed by Yhwh. It would appear that Trito-Isaiah sees the restoration of Zion, even without a political return of the Davidic monarchy, as the fulfillment of God's covenant promises to David. This can be understood as an extended, or even an allegorical, interpretation by Trito-Isaiah of the oracle of the prophet Nathan.

---

[9] The same might be said of Isa 6:13, in which the tenth part of the population, which is likened to a stump left of a fallen tree, is called "holy seed," referring to the ongoing life and regenerative force remaining in the remnant of the people. There is, however, nothing in that passage to indicate that the "seed" is in any way connected to the seed of the Davidic covenant.

After the interjection of the voice of Yhwh in verse 8 (and perhaps 9), the chapter concludes with an exultant hymn in which the prophet (speaking now perhaps on behalf of Jerusalem) rejoices in Yhwh for having clothed him (or her as Zion) with garments of victory.[10] The comparison is made with both a bridegroom and a bride clothed in their wedding garments. A second metaphor is added in verse 11, where the victory of Yhwh is likened to plant growth springing up from the earth. The two metaphors complement the metaphor of light with which the central panel of Trito-Isaiah began in Isaiah 60:1.[11] The wedding garments evoke the splendor, beauty, and glory found also in the dawning light, while the plants sprouting up suggest the unseen suddenness with which God's salvation breaks upon the scene, similar to the crack of dawn.

Verse 10 in particular is significant for how it shifts so easily from one metaphor to another by means of a common linking element. The common element is that of investiture, which appears in the four successive lines after the initial exclamation of rejoicing and exultation in Yhwh. The source of this joy is the action of clothing (*lbš*), wrapping (*ʿṭh*), acting [i.e., vesting] like a priest (*khn*), and adorning (*ʿdh*). In the middle of the clothing imagery, however, the nature of this action changes. The first two lines speak of clothing with garments of salvation (*yšʿ*) and righteousness/victory (*ṣdqh*). The image is of the vested warrior, evoking what was already described of Yhwh in Isaiah 59:17. Indeed, the two verbs *lbš* and *ʿṭh*, along with the two nouns *yšʿ* and *ṣdqh*, are used in each passage.

---

[10] The question regarding the speaker in verse 10 is unclear. Some recent commenters have argued that it must be the prophet himself (Sekine, *Tritojesajanische Sammlung*, 87; Wolfgang Lau, *Schriftgelehrte Prophetie in Jes 56–66: Eine Untersuchung zu den literarischen Bezügen in den letzten elf Kapiteln des Jesajabuches*, BZAW 225 [Berlin: Walter de Gruyter, 1994], 86–87). Others claim it is those who mourn over Zion (Isa 61:2-3) as the anonymous worshipers of this "thanksgiving psalm" into whose mouths the prophet places these words (Blenkinsopp, *Isaiah 56–66*, 230–31). The use of male and female imagery would seem to argue for a both/and solution. The adornment of the bride recalls other bridal and clothing imagery in Isaiah that specifically refers to Jerusalem/Zion (Isa 49:18; 52:1; 62:5). One may also note Isa 54:5, for although the feminine addressee is not named, the larger context makes clear that she is a city (Isa 54:11-12), which is undoubtedly Zion.

[11] Suggestions that these metaphors are somehow incompatible (and therefore evidence of verse 10 being an insertion or verse 11 being an addendum) fail to see the relationship between these metaphors and the root metaphor of light. Duhm's suggestion that verse 10 was an insertion (Duhm, *Das Buch Jesaja*, 458) was taken up by Westermann among others (Westermann, *Isaiah 40–66*, 370–71). Blenkinsopp gives an argument for viewing verse 11 as an appendix based on the jarring metaphorical juxtaposition but ultimately argues for the verse's role as concluding reflection akin to Isa 55:10-11 (Blenkinsopp, *Isaiah 56–66*, 230).

The difference is that what was then ascribed to Yhwh is now ascribed to the prophet/people clothed by Yhwh. This is another example of the mediatory or sacramental role that the prophet, the people, and the city of Jerusalem play in Trito-Isaiah's theology. At the beginning of the Trito-Isaian core, Yhwh's light shone upon Jerusalem so that she herself might be a light to nations and kings (Isa 60:1-2). Now Yhwh's garments of salvation and righteousness become those of the prophet/people/city, once more with a view to "all the nations" (Isa 61:11).

The warrior imagery of verse 10a is transformed into wedding imagery in the last two lines of the verse. It is still a process of robing, but the accoutrements are now those of bridegroom and bride. The double gender in the imagery perhaps illustrates once more that the prophet is speaking both with regard to himself personally and on behalf of the people collectively taken up under the image of daughter Zion. This imagery, which makes a connection between Zion and a wedding celebration, will be explicitly developed in the following chapter.

ISAIAH 62

Prophetic Zeal for Jerusalem, Yhwh's Bride: Isaiah 62:1-7

Isaiah 62 opens with the prophet's pledge to be neither silent nor still until the *ṣdqh* (the righteousness/victory) of Jerusalem is realized.[1] This aspect of the prophetic ministry is then echoed in verse 6, which speaks of guards (*šmrym*) being set on the walls of Jerusalem. These too shall neither be silent nor take rest. The repetition of the verb *ḥšh* in verses 1 and 6 (negated in each case) emphasizes the prophetic office of speaking. The prophetic compulsion to speak is similar to that described in Jeremiah 20:9, except that here it is the object of prophecy—Jerusalem—rather than the word of Yhwh itself that principally motivates the prophet. One may also make a comparison to Ezekiel's portrayal of the prophet as a watchman whose role is to speak up and warn the people (see Ezek 3:17). The difference again here in Trito-Isaiah is that the *šmrym* who are also called "the ones who remind [*hmmzkrym*] Yhwh" in verse 6 are speaking not to the people, but to Yhwh.[2] The prophetic ministry has been turned on its head, so to speak, as the prophet rouses

---

[1] The LXX has 1cs suffixes instead of 3fs suffixes in this verse (i.e., "my righteousness" and "my salvation"). Apparently the Greek translation understands the words as being those of Yhwh and not the prophet. See David A. Baer, *When We All Go Home: Translation and Theology in LXX Isaiah 56–66*, JSOTSup 318, The Hebrew Bible and Its Versions 1 (Sheffield, UK: Sheffield Academic Press, 2001), 71–72.

[2] It appears that the term *mzkrym* ("ones reminding") is based on an actual historical officer whose job it was to record significant matters so that they are not forgotten (see 2 Sam 8:16 and Isa 36:3).The oral rather than the scribal focus here, however, is more evocative of an extrabiblical parallel. There is the story in Herodotus's *Histories* 5.105 of the Persian official who three times daily reminded King Darius not to forget the injury done the Persians by the Athenians (see Blenkinsopp, *Isaiah 56–66*, 239).

Yhwh rather than the people to take decisive action for the restoration and vindication of Jerusalem.

While it appears fairly clear that in verses 6-7 the task of the watchmen and the remembrancers who do not keep silence is to speak to Yhwh, this is not self-evident in the opening verse. The prophetic role as intermediary between God and humans cuts both ways. The prophet may be speaking up to rouse the people or to rouse God. Or, since the prophet speaks in the name of Yhwh, this could even be understood as a statement by Yhwh that he will not remain silent and inactive but rather intervene on behalf of Jerusalem. This seems to be the understanding reflected in LXX.[3] R. N. Whybray notes that this understanding is also consistent with the first-person usage of the verb *ḥšh* in the mouth of Yhwh in Isaiah 42:14; 57:11; and 65:6. These passages refer to Yhwh's past silence/inactivity in contrast to his coming intervention. One may also note that, if Isaiah 62:1 is indeed the voice of Yhwh, this proclamation is an anticipatory response to the prophet's/people's prayer in Isaiah 64:11: "Will you remain silent and let us be afflicted so greatly?"

If it is the voice of the prophet in verse 1, that voice continues in verses 2-5 where Jerusalem is addressed in the second person and Yhwh/God is spoken of in the third person.[4] The theme of salvation/triumph (*yšwʿh*) paired with righteousness/victory (*ṣdq*) carried over from Isaiah 61:10 and reintroduced in Isaiah 62:1b is now further developed. The language of victory is closely conjoined with the language of light. Isaiah 62:1 promised that Zion's righteousness/victory would go forth like brightness (*ngh*) and her salvation/triumph like a torch (*lpyd*) that burns. The latter term is also used to describe lightning as in the theophany on Sinai (Exod 20:15). The visibility of salvation, described in metaphors of light, is further emphasized in Isaiah 62:2a as nations and all kings will see Yhwh's righteousness/victory and glory. The term *ṣdq*, as we have seen, is typically paired with *mšpṭ* when the emphasis is on moral imperative and paired with *yšwʿh* when the emphasis is on God's act of vindication. Here, where the salvific denotation is clear from verse 1, it is paired with glory (*kbwd*). Zion's victory is conceived as a manifestation of radiant light visible to the ends of the earth.[5]

The imagery of light present at the beginning of chapter 62 recalls the light at the beginning of chapter 60, where the glory of Yhwh shone

---

[3] This is also the position taken by Pierre E. Bonnard (*Le Second Isaïe: Son disciple et leurs éditeurs Isaïe 40–66*, EBib [Paris: Gabalda, 1972], 425) and Whybray (*Isaiah 40–66*, 246–47).

[4] Whybray (*Isaiah 40–66*, 246) would see verses 2-5 as a prophetic comment on the divine speech of verse 1, with a return to divine speech in verse 6.

[5] This also echoes Isaiah 58:8, where images of light and victory were combined.

upon the people of Jerusalem. These, in turn, were called to shine as well, so that nations and kings might walk to their light. This image of Jerusalem becoming a beacon or a light to the nations (see Isa 49:6) will culminate at the end of the book, where it is said that all the nations shall be gathered and come to Jerusalem to behold Yhwh's glory (Isa 66:18-20). There is something of a chain reaction in the thought of Trito-Isaiah. The glory of Yhwh shines on Zion so that her glory may in turn shine on the nations, leading them back to her to behold the glory of Yhwh in Zion. The ministerial role of Zion in the unfolding of Yhwh's salvation in Trito-Isaiah (and one might add Deutero- and Proto-Isaiah as well) is clearly stated through the use of these metaphors of light.

The many words for light (*'wr*), radiance (*ngh*), splendor (*tp'rt*), and glory (*kbwd*) that are used in Trito-Isaiah, especially in the central chapters of 60–62, are used so frequently as metaphors for salvation that they come to be used as synonyms for the realities of justice (*mšpt*), righteousness (*ṣdqh*), salvation (*yšwʿh*), and well-being (*šlwm*) that they represent. In fact, they become interchangeable with Yhwh himself. From the very beginning of these chapters we saw light identified with the glory of Yhwh (Isa 60:1) and indeed Yhwh's very self (Isa 60:2). So when we hear that nations and kings will see the *ṣdqh* and *kbwd* of Jerusalem in Isaiah 62:2, we need to recall that this is the visible light of Yhwh's salvation—Yhwh himself—that is seen. This anticipates the final chapter of the book, in which Yhwh proclaims the gathering of all nations to behold "my glory" (Isa 66:18).

That final gathering of the nations will be located, of course, in Zion. The centrality of Jerusalem, so prominent in the thought of First, Second, and Third Isaiah, is also emphasized here inasmuch as it is *her* righteousness/victory and *her* glory that are spoken of in Isaiah 62:1. The use of the second-person, feminine, singular possessive pronouns shows that Yhwh's gift is also Zion's possession. While the second half of Isaiah 62:2 emphasizes Yhwh as the source of Jerusalem's victory and glory, unlike Isaiah 58:8 (where the imagery of light/glory came to the fore in Third Isaiah) and Isaiah 66:18-20 (where the imagery reaches its climax), here the glory that shines for all to see is attributed directly to Jerusalem.[6] What is ascribed to Yhwh elsewhere belongs here to Yhwh's holy city, Jerusalem. Of course, it is important to remember that "your glory" is also identified with "your God" (see Isa 60:19). The glory, like the new name, is certainly understood as the gift of Yhwh, since it is Yhwh himself who will bring about the restoration and exaltation of Jerusalem (Isa 62:7).

---

[6] There will be one further passage, in Isa 66:11, in which glory is directly attributed to Jerusalem.

The giving of a new name is a common biblical motif closely associated with personal transformation of identity and mission. The renaming of Jerusalem hearkens back to the first part of the book of Isaiah, where Yhwh promises a purification and refining of Jerusalem, after which "you shall be called city of righteousness [*'yr ḥṣdq*], city of faithfulness" (Isa 1:26). Likewise, the prophet Jeremiah (Jer 33:16) had spoken of a new name for Jerusalem—"Yhwh our righteousness" (*yhwh ṣdqnw*).[7] Now that Third Isaiah speaks of the "righteousness" of Jerusalem that is about to shine forth (Isa 62:1) and be seen by the nations (Isa 62:2), it seems clear that this new name is also alluding to the passages of First Isaiah and Jeremiah. Just as the glory that belongs to Yhwh is here attributed to Jerusalem, so too the righteousness that Jeremiah had identified with Yhwh in Jerusalem's new name is more directly applied to the city itself in Third Isaiah. Jerusalem is becoming more closely identified with Yhwh and his glory and righteousness through the transformative renewal that Yhwh is about to accomplish in her.

Third Isaiah will put his own stamp on the new name of Jerusalem in the following verses. Whereas "the city of righteousness" and "Yhwh our righteousness," which First Isaiah and Jeremiah spoke of, are unmistakably alluded to in the focus on Jerusalem's righteousness/victory in the opening verses of Isaiah 62, the name that is finally pronounced in verse 4 will tie in more explicitly with the marital imagery that is beginning to unfold in this chapter. The progressively shifting metaphors of Trito-Isaiah lead us from triumph and victory, through light and glory, to exaltation and espousal. Just as the renamed city is not original with Trito-Isaiah, so too the marriage of Yhwh to his land, people, or city has a long pedigree that reaches back through the prophetic texts of Deutero-Isaiah, Ezekiel, and Jeremiah all the way to Hosea in the eighth century. But here too Trito-Isaiah will introduce his own innovations into the well-established metaphor.

In Isaiah 62:3, the symbolism of Jerusalem's vindication and exaltation shifts from that of shining light to royal jewelry. One may note, however, that light remains even in this new image as the genitive con-

---

[7] Ezekiel also gives a new name to Jerusalem in 48:35: "Yhwh is there." So the theme of the renaming of a restored Jerusalem is found across the Major Prophets. Trito-Isaiah appears to have especially in mind the passages from First Isaiah and Jeremiah where this name is connected to righteousness, which has been mentioned twice already in verses 1-2 with respect to Jerusalem. Although Trito-Isaiah does not call Jerusalem by this name, the idea permeates all of Trito-Isaiah and is especially concentrated at the end of chapter 61 and the beginning of chapter 62. See George A. F. Knight, *The New Israel: A Commentary on the Book of Isaiah 56–66* (Grand Rapids, MI: Eerdmans, 1985), 62–63.

struction describes a shining or glorious crown (*ʿṭrt tpʾrt*). The beauty, splendor, or glory signified by *tpʾrt* closely parallels the luminous manifestation of *kbwd* from the previous verse. Commentators have noted the peculiarity of the crown being in the hand rather than upon the head.[8] One likely proposal is that the shifting imagery in the surrounding verses is all thematically connected around the root metaphor of marriage, which will become explicit in the following verses. That is to say that the crown in verse 3, as well as the new name in verse 2, are elements that can be understood in light of an ancient Israelite wedding.[9] Song of Songs 3:11 refers to the crown (*ʿṭrh*) that Solomon's mother gave to him on his wedding day. There is also mention in *Pirqe Rabbi Eliezer* (16) of the marital custom, while the temple still stood, by which bride and bridegroom wore crowns during the ceremony and were addressed as "the king" and "the queen."[10] This text, like Isaiah 62:2-5, closely associates marriage, crowning, and reception of a new name. Similarly, Eastern Christians are familiar with a crowning rite that has been a part of their marriage ceremonies for centuries.[11] The presence of the crown in the hand of Yhwh could then be understood in the sense that Yhwh is about to crown Jerusalem in a symbolic ritual action that makes her his bride. It does seem that, considering the organically evolving metaphors that flow one into another in Trito-Isaiah, verse 3 is a transitional link between the preceding triumphal imagery and the spousal imagery that follows. A comparison between this verse and Isaiah 61:10, which also contained spousal imagery, reveals that in the earlier passage the city/prophet was adorned with wedding garments, while in the present verse the city is identified with the ornamentation itself.[12]

[8] E.g., Whybray, *Isaiah 40–66*, 247; Jan L. Koole, *Isaiah III*, vol. 3: *Isaiah 56–66*, Historical Commentary on the Old Testament (Leuven: Peeters, 1997), 306–7.

[9] Koole, *Isaiah III*, 306.

[10] See Blenkinsopp, *Isaiah 56–66*, 236–37.

[11] Although scholars debate the origins of the crowning ceremony in Eastern Orthodox Christianity, Gary Vikan ("Art and Marriage in Early Byzantium," in *Dumbarton Oaks Papers*, vol. 44 [Cambridge, MA: Harvard University Press, 1990], 145–63) has argued for a pre-Christian Roman origin that was popularized by the Greeks. This may be indicative of a broader cross-cultural practice shared by Second Temple Judaism.

[12] This peculiarity could work against Koole's interpretation, which sees in verse 3 a marital crowning ceremony. Jerusalem does not receive the crown, but rather she is the crown. This is also pointed out by Whybray (*Isaiah 40–66*, 247), who suggests that Jerusalem is a crown to be worn by Yhwh. He notes the physical resemblance of her city walls to a tiara and the oft-cited Babylonian text in which an address to Bel (Marduk) states: "Borsippa [the city] is thy tiara" (*ANET*, 331). But this brings one back to the first difficulty: the fact that the crown is in the hand, not on the head.

As with the focus on light, vindication/righteousness, and glory in verses 1-2, verse 3 uses imagery that closely identifies Jerusalem with Yhwh. Jerusalem is described as royal jewels in the hand of Yhwh. Just as the new name came to her from the mouth of Yhwh, her new royal status comes as a gift from Yhwh's hand. The splendor that the city shall possess is thus in no way independent of Yhwh but rather completely dependent on his graciousness. The confluence of Jerusalem's name and Yhwh's hand in these verses also calls to mind Isaiah 49:16 and the unfathomable bond of intimacy that is expressed between Yhwh and Jerusalem there.

In fact, there are numerous allusions between Isaiah 62:1-6 and Isaiah 49:14-19. It will be instructive to list them:

Zion	Isaiah 49:14	Isaiah 62:1
forsaken (ʿzb)	Isaiah 49:14	Isaiah 62:4
palm (kp)	Isaiah 49:16	Isaiah 62:3
your walls (ḥwmtyk)	Isaiah 49:16	Isaiah 62:6
sons/builders (bnym)[13]	Isaiah 49:17	Isaiah 62:5
bride (clh)	Isaiah 49:18	Isaiah 62:5
desolate (šmmh)	Isaiah 49:19	Isaiah 62:4

In addition to these verbal correspondences, there are also further implied and thematic links between the two passages. For example, although Zion's name (šm) which is so prominent in Isaiah 62:1-5 is not mentioned in Isaiah 49:14-19, it can be understood that this is

[13] What might be the most significant connection between these passages is the fact that they both employ a deliberate pun on the terms "children" and "builder(s)"— the consonantal texts of which are identical. In Isa 49:17, bnyk may be read as "your builders" or "your sons." While MT points the text as "your sons," 1QIsaᵃ has a plene spelling (bwnyk) indicating "your builders." The Vulgate and Aquila agree with the vocalization of the text suggested by 1QIsaᵃ. The surrounding context makes a strong argument for reading the term both ways. The last line of the preceding verse reads: "your walls are before me always," to which the arrival of builders is the logical response. The following verses speak of "jewels" adorning Jerusalem and the arrival of many people crowding Jerusalem, all of which suggests children. While there is no similar variation among the ancient versions with regard to the text of Isa 62:5 (universally reading "your sons"), the consonantal text is equally ambiguous, as we shall see.

what Yhwh is scratching out when he says "I have engraved *you* on my palms." Similarly, the crown and diadem of Isaiah 62:3 are particular items that fall under the more generic term "jewels" or "ornaments" (*ʿdy*) of Isaiah 49:18.[14]

The intimate and passionate relationship that is expressed between Yhwh and a Zion that is in the process of being redeemed and transformed takes a somewhat different tack in Isaiah 62 as compared to Isaiah 49. There, the relational imagery was that of mother and child, whereas here it is the language of bridegroom and bride.[15] The coming vindication that the prophet announced at the beginning of this chapter is now described in terms of a wedding between Jerusalem and Yhwh. Marital imagery for the relationship between Yhwh and his people is not a new concept with Third Isaiah, as has been noted. One can trace the imagery from Hosea through Jeremiah and Ezekiel and into Second Isaiah before coming to the present text. The pan-Isaian emphasis on the city of Jerusalem follows the innovation of Ezekiel in identifying the bride of Yhwh not simply as the people of Israel (as earlier in Hos 1–3 and Jer 2–3) but more precisely as the city of Jerusalem itself.[16]

We have been noting the many verbal and thematic connections between Second and Third Isaiah. The movement between these sections of the book of Isaiah is in many ways a subtle one. The restoration and exaltation of Jerusalem is foremost among the themes uniting chapters 40–66. Having already noted the many allusions between chapters 49 and 62, we can now turn our attention to other antecedents in Deutero-Isaiah that presage the marital imagery that—while perhaps implied in Isaiah 62:2-3—becomes explicit in Isaiah 62:4. Continuing the direct-address speech that began in verse 2, Jerusalem is still being addressed by the prophet in Isaiah 62:4. "Never again shall you be called 'Forsaken'

[14] In addition to the lexical and thematic connections between Isa 49:14-19 and Isa 62:1-6, it has also been observed that there is an entire phrase from Isa 49:18 that is repeated verbatim in the core of Trito-Isaiah (Isa 60:4): "Lift up your eyes and look around; they all gather together, they come to you." Risto Nurmela, *The Mouth of the Lord Has Spoken: Inner-Biblical Allusions in Second and Third Isaiah*, Studies in Judaism (Lanham, MD: University Press of America, 2006), 55. While this passage does not directly relate to Isa 62, it once again points to an especially close connection between Isa 60–62 and Isa 40–55.

[15] This difference need not be taken as an argument for the different authorship of Deutero- and Trito-Isaiah. That a single prophet may use both images was already demonstrated by Hosea (Hos 1–3, 11).

[16] Jeremiah 2:2 does have the prophet speaking his words to Jerusalem, but as the chapter unfolds the addressee is clearly seen to be Israel (Jer 2:3) and the house of Jacob (Jer 2:4), with the narrative including a much broader scope than the city of Jerusalem (e.g., the time in the wilderness in Jer 2:2).

[ʿzwbh], nor shall your land be called 'Deserted' [šmmh]." The abandoned and deserted wife had been previously encountered in Isaiah 50:1 and especially 54:1-8 (where the same contrast between šmmh and bʿwlh is made). She is here once more addressed and once more reminded that her lot is about to be permanently changed. The spousal metaphor taken up by Second Isaiah is continued in the third part of the book as a primary image that is now used to speak of the joy and exaltation of a renewed Jerusalem.

Given the similarities between these passages, Isaiah 54:1-8 bears a little closer examination. Isaiah 54:1 opens with an address to the "barren woman" (ʿqrh). This woman, who is described as not having given birth (yldh) and not having labored (ḥlh), is also called "desolate" or "deserted" (šmmh). The three prior descriptors indicate that the term šmmh is related to childlessness, while the comparison made in the last part of the verse ("For the children of the deserted one will be more than the children of the espoused") sees the term as related to marital status.[17] Although the two concepts are closely related—since an abandoned wife is unlikely to produce children—Isaiah 54:1 plays on a double sense of šmmh, which can be understood as "deserted" by her husband or "barren" of children. One finds a similar double sense in Isaiah 62:4a, where šmmh can be taken in synonymous parallelism with ʿzwbh as referring to the abandoned wife. But it can also be understood as "barrenness" in complementary parallelism to ʿzwbh in that Zion is both without husband and without children.

We have already noted that Isaiah 54:1 makes the same contrast between the abandoned/barren wife (šmmh) and the espoused wife (bʿwlh) as Isaiah 62:4. In the passage from Deutero-Isaiah, however, they were compared as different entities. From the context, it seems clear that Zion was referred to by the former term, while the latter appears to be a generic term of contrast and comparison. The prophet was saying that there will be a future reversal of the present situation whereby the children of Zion (now barren) will surpass those of the espoused wife. In Isaiah 62:4 both terms are used of Zion as her name changes from "abandoned" (ʿzwbh) and "deserted" (šmmh) to "I delight in her" (ḥpṣybh) and "espoused" (bʿwlh). It may simply be coincidental that two of the four names mentioned in this verse are found elsewhere in the Bible

---

[17] Here, as in Isa 62:4, Whybray (*Isaiah 40–66*, 248) understands the term as simply referring to barrenness. Although the emphasis in Isa 54 is certainly on childlessness giving way to the bearing of children and the increase in population, Isa 62 focuses much more on the espousal or wedding of Zion as Yhwh her husband takes her back and delights in her. Oddly, even the one mention of children in verse 5 refers to them as marrying (bʿl) Zion.

as proper names, both of them the mothers of kings. Azubah was the mother of Jehoshaphat (1 Kgs 22:42) and Hephzibah was the mother of Manasseh (2 Kgs 21:1). This coincidence does at least point out, however, that the names mentioned here are plausible as proper names, even if their translations don't strike us as such.

A final key point of comparison to take from Isaiah 54 sheds light on a difficult passage in Isaiah 62:5. Isaiah 54:5 reads, "For your maker will espouse you; / Yhwh Sabaoth is his name. / The Holy One of Israel will redeem you; / He is called God of all the earth." This verse clearly refers to Yhwh marrying the abandoned wife who is understood to be Zion.[18] In describing this marriage or espousal, the verb *bʿl* is used of Yhwh. Furthermore, Yhwh is identified as "your maker," using the suffixed form of the active participle of the verb "to make" (*ʿśyk*). Each of these points will be significant as we turn our attention to Isaiah 62:5.

At the risk of "violating the rules" of a commentary focused on the received text, it is necessary to mention a textual emendation that many scholars and translators make that has been followed here. This would render Isaiah 62:5a: "As a young man marries a virgin / Your builder will marry you." The Masoretic text as well as all of the ancient versions read "your sons" instead of "your builder" in Isaiah 62:5. Given the absence of textual witnesses, an explanation is in order for translating "your builder" (*bōnēk* or possibly *bōnayik*) where MT has *bānāyik*. First of all, a textual-critical explanation for the change from *bnk* to *bnyk* is readily at hand. The orthographic similarity could easily lead a scribe to mistake "your builder" for the much more common "your sons." In the second place, the text as it stands would create a bizarre and unseemly metaphor, with sons marrying their mother.[19] Third, the poetic parallelism in the verse seems to require that the noun in question in 5a correspond to "your God" in 5b. "Your builder" satisfies this requirement, while "your sons" does not.[20] Finally "your builder" fits in better

---

[18] This contradicts the assertion of Elizabeth Achtemeier (*The Community and Message of Isaiah 56–66* [Minneapolis: Augsburg, 1982], 98), who, commenting on Isa 62:5, claims "the marriage of the god to his country was a distinctly Canaanite mythological usage; the god was the ʿbaʾal,ʾ husband and owner, of the land. . . . The Old Testament usually avoids such pagan concepts as it does here in verse 5."

[19] Francis Andersen explains the reading in MT as a contamination of the symbolism of Yhwh and the returning exiles as Jerusalem's bridegroom. Many other scholars suggest translating *bʿl* here as "to possess" rather than "to marry." See Koole, *Isaiah III*, 310–11.

[20] To argue for a "progressive parallelism" (whereby "your sons" need not correspond to "your God") rather than a more synonymous one in this verse does violence

with the surrounding theme of the restoration and reconstruction of Jerusalem. It is in fact Yhwh who will establish or found (*kwn*, Polel) Jerusalem in verse 7.

A final point that can be made to justify the reading of "your builder," against the universal witness of manuscripts and ancient versions reading "your sons," is that the consonantal text as it stands (without recourse to emendation) may very well read "your builder." The Hebrew verb *bnh*, like other III-*He* verbs in Hebrew, actually has a *yod* rather than a *he* as its third root consonant. In general, this *yod* appears only in passive participle forms, while the reading of "your builder" would be an active participle. It is also the case, however, that the final *yod* appears "in certain rare forms, especially in pause."[21] It so happens that *bnyk* is in pause at the end of the first colon of verse 5. The word is marked by an *atnah* in the Masoretic text, clearly indicating its pausal position at the middle of the verse. So the consonantal Hebrew text of Isaiah 62:5 is ambiguous. The four consonants *bnyk* could be a pausal form of the standard *bnk* ("your builder"). Since this pausal form is identical to the consonants for "your sons," the widespread misreading, which gravitates toward the far more common noun, is easily explained.[22] One may also note that the suffixed III-*He* participle here (*bnyk*) follows the same pattern as the masculine, singular, suffixed III-*He* participle in Isaiah 54:5 (*^csyk*) where there is no question of it being a singular form, since Israel has only one maker and there is no plural noun with which it might be easily confused. Whatever one concludes about how to read this verse, it is clear that Trito-Isaiah utilizes deliberate wordplay, mixing sounds as he mixes imagery. Both children and rebuilding are prominent themes throughout the text, and, indeed, they are interrelated. For the rebuilding of Zion is a matter not simply of physical construction but of repopulation as well. Nevertheless, the logic of poetry as well as the logic of imagery (supported by an awareness of the scribal tendency to misread

---

to the text. The entire series of bicola in Isa 62:1-5 have a rather tight synonymous parallelism with each of the elements of the first line being repeated in the second. Verse 5 would not fit into this literary pattern if one reads "your sons," which in no way corresponds to "your God." Note also that in Isa 54:5, which follows a similar structure, "your maker will marry you" is paralleled with "the Holy one of Israel will redeem you."

[21] Paul Joüon and Takamitsu Muraoka, *A Grammar of Biblical Hebrew*, 3rd reprint of the 2nd ed., with corrections (Rome: Gregorian and Biblical Press, 2011), 189.

[22] Less easy to explain is the plural verbal form *yb^clwk*. It would seem that here emendation would be required, removing the *vav* to arrive at the required masculine singular verb. One would need to argue that a scribal misreading of *bnyk* as "your sons" instead of "your builder" prompted the scribal "correction" of *yb^clk* to *yb^clwk*.

a more common word in place of a rarer one) argue strongly for reading the present verse as "Your Builder will marry you."

Returning to the imagery of this passage, we may note that the more systematic studies of marital imagery in the Bible generally give little or no attention to Isaiah 62:4-5.[23] This is somewhat surprising in light of its repeated assertions that Yhwh will marry Jerusalem. In fact, the verb "to

---

[23] Richtsje Abma (*Bonds of Love: Methodic Studies of Prophetic Texts with Marriage Imagery [Isaiah 50:1-3 and 54:1-10, Hosea 1–3, Jeremiah 2–3]* [Assen: Van Gorcum, 1999], 5) excludes it from her study, but with a much less substantial argument than for her exclusion of Ezek 16 and 23. It is unclear to me why her stated criterion that "texts cannot simply be removed from their literary context in order to study the treatment of one particular theme" disqualifies Isa 62 any more than it would the texts she does examine. Gerlinde Baumann (*Love and Violence: Marriage as Metaphor for the Relationship between YHWH and Israel in the Prophetic Books* [Collegeville, MN: Liturgical Press, 2003], 188–89) treats the passage in less than a full page, even though, by her own admission, the text has a unique density of the use of the verb to marry (*bꜥl*) in the Old Testament. One suspects that the slight treatment is connected to the fact that Isa 62 does not support her thesis that "imagery of violent sexual abuse [is] an essential element in marital imagery" (p. 226). Or as restated two pages later: "YHWH's punishing violence is a necessary element in the prophetic marriage imagery" (p. 228). Renita Weems (*Battered Love: Marriage, Sex, and Violence in the Hebrew Prophets* [Minneapolis: Fortress Press, 1995]) likewise ignores any treatment of the marital metaphor in Isaiah, while addressing Hosea, Jeremiah, and Ezekiel. While the exclusion may be due to the intentional focus of her study on violence in connection with the marital metaphor (as is also the case with Baumann), it creates a methodological flaw by which she concludes (similarly to Baumann) that sexual violence is an inseparable part of the marital metaphor. Isa 62 clearly demonstrates that this is not the case.

Raymond C. Ortlund Jr. (*Whoredom: God's Unfaithful Wife in Biblical Theology*, New Studies in Biblical Theology [Grand Rapids, MI: Eerdmans, 1996) likewise excludes the passages in Isaiah from his study, but he is at least more clear in the title of his work that he is dealing precisely with the image of whoredom or infidelity and not marriage per se. He writes: "In Is.50:1, 54:4-6 and 62:5 marital language is used, but the theme of Israel's harlotry is not developed" (p. 77n1). He thus avoids the erroneous conclusion that marriage is a necessarily violent image in biblical prophecy.

The other recent work of which I am aware that offers a systematic treatment of the marriage metaphor across the prophetic corpus is: Teresa Solà, *Jahvè, Espos d'Israel: Poderosa Metàfora Profètica* (Barcelona: Claret, 2006). This work was unavailable to me at the time of this writing.

Sometimes, monographs, focused on one particular instance of marital imagery in the Bible, will give a brief overview of the marriage metaphor in the prophets. In these cases as well, it is not unusual to find Isa 62 left out or marginalized. See, e.g., Julie Galambush (*Jerusalem in the Book of Ezekiel: The City as Yahweh's Wife* [Atlanta: Scholars Press, 1992], 59n102), who very briefly discusses texts from Deutero-Isaiah, focusing oddly on Isa 51 along with Isa 54, but relegates Isa 62 to a single sentence in a footnote.

marry" (*bʿl*) occurs four times in just these two verses.[24] From its frequent usage, it would appear that any negative associations of the root *bʿl* with Baalism are not problematic for Trito-Isaiah as they were for Hosea. The prophet freely uses the word to speak of the joyful reunion of Yhwh and Jerusalem. The key element that is missing from these verses when compared with the other prophetic texts that use the marriage metaphor is the negative characterization of Israel/Jerusalem as the faithless wife. In Isaiah 62, Jerusalem's punishment of being forsaken and deserted (without any mention of the sins for which she was punished) is referred to as a thing in the past, but the focus of the passage is on the marriage of Yhwh and Jerusalem as a joyful event.[25] "As a bridegroom rejoices over a bride, your God rejoices over you" (Isa 62:5b). The marital metaphor understood in this light becomes for Trito-Isaiah a very appropriate image for denoting the glorious transformation of Jerusalem to a new and exalted status. Trito-Isaiah does not use marriage to tell the story of Israel's crime and punishment as his predecessors did. He does not even use it to highlight Yhwh's mercy and forgiveness as the long-suffering, abandoned husband. Instead, marriage becomes the vehicle for expressing Yhwh's delight in his people and the joyful exaltation of Jerusalem.

If Isaiah 62 breaks the mold of biblical prophecies utilizing marital imagery, perhaps the mold as constructed was not the right shape to begin with. Drawn to the often shocking portrayal of whoring Israel/Jerusalem and the graphic descriptions of her punishment, scholars have tended to define the metaphor as "the adulterous wife"[26] or as "God's unfaithful wife."[27] Often focused on the roles of economic and social realities in shaping and defining ancient marriages, they have been prone to neglect the fact that, then as now, a marriage could also be cause for spousal delight and rejoicing. Concerned (and rightly so) about the potential "reverse action" of imagery in shaping our views of the metaphorical vehicles

---

[24] As was earlier noted, Hosea avoids the use of the term in connection with Yhwh's marriage to Israel. It is found in Jer 3:14, but with some question about its marital connotation there since Yhwh is addressing children, not wife, in his rapidly shifting metaphors. It is also found in Jer 31:32, where a covenant context is clear, but marital imagery is not. Here in Isaiah, used in conjunction with *btwlh* and *klh*, the marital implications are not in doubt.

[25] It is likely that the entire history of the metaphor was implicitly understood inasmuch as Isa 62 is a prophecy about a reversal of fortunes. Still, it is noteworthy that the prophet makes no explicit mention of any crimes of Jerusalem, and she is not characterized as being or having been faithless or adulterous. Indeed, far from being compared to a *znh* or a *nʾpt*, she is likened to a *btwlh*.

[26] Baumann, *Love and Violence*, 29.

[27] Ortlund, *Whoredom*.

(the imagery used—in this case marriage), they have stopped short of fully realizing the metaphor's original purpose in elucidating the tenor (the reality symbolized by the imagery—here Yhwh's relationship to Jerusalem/Israel).[28]

Verses 6 and 7 return to the theme of the prophetic watchmen, whose job it is to speak not to the people but to Yhwh regarding Jerusalem's restoration. This forms an inclusio with the opening verse of the chapter, sandwiching the imagery of Jerusalem as Yhwh's resplendent and vindicated bride. The twenty-four-hour vigilance of the watchmen has as its goal the urging of Yhwh to act on Jerusalem's behalf. It is the rarer intercessory role of the prophet (see Gen 20:7), speaking to God rather than appealing to humans, that is once again highlighted here in Isaiah 62. It is interesting that the role of the watchmen (*šmrym*) stationed on Jerusalem's walls is not to watch for potential enemies but to implore Yhwh incessantly to restore Jerusalem.[29] The use of the imagery of watchmen here does not therefore mirror the imagery of Ezekiel's sentinel (*zph*) whose role it is to announce things to come. Rather, Trito-Isaiah emphasizes another meaning associated with watchmen—that of patient endurance as they eagerly await the end of their watch. Psalm 130:6-7 uses the watchmen imagery in a similar fashion as a metaphor for eagerly waiting for Yhwh. With a further twist here, Trito-Isaiah has the watchmen eagerly implore Yhwh without rest, highlighting the vigilance associated with watchmen.

The fact that these watchmen are also called *mzkrym* ("remembrancers") leads to further questions about their identification. Since the *mzkyr* was a royal official (2 Sam 8:16; Isa 36:3), it would make sense that Yhwh, as king, would appoint his royal officials and hence be the speaker of Isaiah 62:6 (or at least 62:6a). Furthermore, since Yhwh's heavenly court is populated by angelic ministers, some would see these *mzkrym* as heavenly beings whom the prophet is imploring in Isaiah 62:6b. One sees a similar role exercised by the angel of Yhwh in Zechariah 1:12.[30] While

---

[28] Baumann, *Love and Violence*, 35–36. Baumann's work is typical in this regard. She expresses two very valid concerns behind her book: that the prophetic marital imagery can shape a hierarchical view of marital relationships and legitimate the use of marital violence as punishment.

[29] In light of this, the question may be raised as to who the speaker might be here. It would seem to be the prophet's voice rather than the prophet speaking in Yhwh's name since he calls on the watchmen to give Yhwh no rest. On the other hand, this act of appointment (*pqd*, Hiphil), which is so reminiscent of prophetic calling, seems more proper to Yhwh than to the prophet. It may also be that Isa 62:6a is an interjection by the voice of Yhwh, and Isa 62:6b reverts back to the prophet speaking.

[30] This was the observation and conclusion of Duhm, who saw the *mzkrym* as angelic beings here. His suggestion is noted and rejected by Westermann (*Isaiah 40–66,*

disagreements over the speaker in this passage and the identity of the watchmen/remembrancers remain, the function of the latter is clear. Whether human or angelic, appointed by the prophet or Yhwh himself, they are to constantly urge and incite Yhwh to act on behalf of Jerusalem.

Yhwh's Pledge of Restoration: Isaiah 62:8-12

The response to the entreaties of the watchmen and remembrancers of Yhwh comes quickly. Isaiah 62:8 introduces an oath of Yhwh with rather eschatological implications. Similar to the oath to Noah and his descendants never again to destroy all flesh by the waters of a flood (Gen 9:11), Yhwh here promises never again to subject Jerusalem and its inhabitants to the despoliation of warfare. As with the marital imagery in the preceding verses, there appears to be a dependence on the precedent of Hosea in speaking of the blessings of grain (*dgn*) and new wine (*tyrwš*) as being provided and vouchsafed by Yhwh (see Hos 2:10-11). The oath is given in the conventional manner of later Hebrew writing, which gives only the protasis (literally: "If ever again I give your grain as food to your enemies") while omitting, but implying, the apodosis that would have been some self-imprecation.

Verse 9 adds a cultic context to the acts of eating and drinking the food and wine that the people have with effort produced and that Yhwh has promised not to take from them. This logically follows from verse 8, as the people recognize by their actions that they owe the enjoyment of the fruits of their labors to Yhwh's goodwill toward them. The second half of the verse, which speaks of the drinking of wine "in my holy courts," especially points beyond a mere attitude of thanksgiving to an actual ritual in the temple. This seems to refer to the ancient practice, which was continued in the postexilic period, of offering the firstfruits of the harvest in the temple, at which time those making the offering would also share in it with the priests (see, e.g., Deut 12:17-18; Neh 13:12).

Connections with Deutero-Isaiah (Isa 40:3-4) are once more in evidence as the prophet calls for the clearing of the people's way to Jerusalem and through her gates in verse 10. And even though the path that is cleared is called the way of the people (*drk h'm*), it is the coming of Yhwh about which the prophet speaks in verse 11. Thus, although the

---

377) as improbable. Why would Yhwh appoint angels to give him no rest until he establishes Jerusalem? But given the similar scene in Herodotus (*Histories* 5.105), in which King Darius appoints a servant to constantly remind him of the injury done by the Athenians until he avenges it, perhaps the proposition is not at all improbable.

language is different from Isaiah 40:3, the concept is closely related to the way of Yhwh (*drk yhwh*) that is found there. Some have suggested that "the people" mentioned in this verse are the Gentiles who will come streaming into Jerusalem (see Isa 2:2-4 where the terms "nations" [*gwym*] and "peoples" [*ʿmmym*] are used synonymously in parallel construction).[31] This could be argued from the grammar that here has the definite article rather than the possessive suffix (my people) inasmuch as the definite form refers to people in general in Isaiah 40:7 and 42:5.[32] The context, however, which concludes with a reference to "the holy people, Yhwh's redeemed," seems to demand an understanding that applies the term to the returned exiles of Judah.

The use of double imperatives in verse 10 (*ʿbrw ʿbrw*, "Pass through, pass through!" and *slw slw*, "Build up, build up!") continues the style of the very beginning of Deutero-Isaiah (*nḥmw nḥmw*, "Comfort, comfort!"). Thus, there are stylistic as well as verbal and thematic links running throughout Isaiah 40–66. James Muilenburg, Claus Westermann, and Joseph Blenkinsopp, among others, have all pointed to the close connections between Isaiah 62:10-12 and Deutero-Isaiah.[33] This reinforces the understanding of Isaiah 60–62 as the core of Trito-Isaiah, having as it does the closest literary and thematic connections to Isaiah 40–55. According to this view, these chapters would have also been the earliest to be composed from Isaiah 56–66, being very close to the historical context of Isaiah 40–55.

The construction of the road passing through the gates of Jerusalem completes the picture of the reconstruction and exaltation of the city itself with which the chapter began. The use of the poetic synonym *mslh* for *drk* coupled with the double imperative *slw* doubly connects the way to the city as it is physically and morally raised up. This imagery also connects with the idea of the repopulation of the city as the people pass through the gates so that Jerusalem is no longer an abandoned city (Isa 62:12). But most significantly, it speaks of Yhwh's coming to his holy city, which is announced in verse 11. Throughout the chapter it is Yhwh's return to, and action on behalf of, his city that the prophet has been vigilantly imploring. It is the return of the husband to his bride that is the answer to the prophet's petition. Yhwh's presence can never be entirely separated from what Yhwh is doing on his people's behalf. Yhwh's victorious return is also identified with the return of Yhwh's redeemed. These latter may

---

[31] Knight, *New Israel*, 68–69.

[32] Koole, *Isaiah III*, 321.

[33] Westermann, *Isaiah 40–66*, 378–79, where he also quotes Muilenburg; Blenkinsopp, *Isaiah 56–66*, 242–44.

even be referred to as the "reward" and "recompense" that accompany Zion's bringer of salvation.[34]

The phrase "See, his reward is with him, and his recompense before him" in Isaiah 62:11 is a verbatim repetition of Isaiah 40:10.[35] One difference we see between the phrase in its present context and its earlier appearance is that the immediate antecedent of the masculine singular pronouns in chapter 40 was clearly Yhwh. Here it may be Yhwh (from the opening line of the verse) or "your salvation" (*yšʿk*) that is the more immediate antecedent. The Septuagint, Targums, and Vulgate all read "your savior" for "your salvation," thus identifying the latter with Yhwh. One has to admit that, even following the MT and reading "your salvation," it is difficult to translate the subsequent possessive pronouns impersonally since salvation itself is personified in this case. Reading with MT, we do get a clearer appreciation of Trito-Isaiah's conception of salvation not simply as something that Yhwh does or brings but as the very saving presence of Yhwh himself. Finally, we may note that the repeated line from Deutero-Isaiah reminds us that the salvation of Jerusalem, which is identified with the return of Yhwh her God, is not an isolated event at the end of the Babylonian exile but a recurring or ongoing event in the postexilic reconstruction. The prophet has been praying that Yhwh might fulfill what he has promised and finish what he has begun. And now that fulfillment is announced as imminent. The triple use of *hnnh* in verse 11 gives a sense of temporal immediacy.

The chapter concludes with a reference once more to the new name for Jerusalem that was first promised in verse 2 and explicated in verse 4. The naming of the city (addressed as "you") is here coupled with the naming of its inhabitants ("they"). In Isaiah 62:4 it was the city and the land that were given the names "I delight in her" and "Married." The people are here called "the holy people"—a name that will show up again in the lament of the following chapter (Isa 63:18). They are also called "Yhwh's redeemed"—a fitting title for the people in Third Isaiah with its emphasis on Yhwh as the redeemer of Israel. The final name given to Jerusalem, "city not forsaken," directly refers to the promise in verse 4 that she shall no longer be called "forsaken." The other name, "sought out," unlike the other three names in this verse, does not at first glance

---

[34] Scholars generally understand the initial reference in Isaiah 40:10 to Yhwh's "reward and recompense" as a reference to the returning exiles (see Whybray, *Isaiah 40–66*, 52). Some continue the identification in this passage as well, while others see a more immediate and logical connection to the salvation that Yhwh brings to Zion mentioned in the same verse (see Koole, *Isaiah III*, 325).

[35] Nurmela (*Mouth of the Lord*, 119–20) highlights this as yet another sign of the close connections between Isa 62:10-12 and Isa 40–55.

appear to have any direct connections to the immediate passage or to the broader context of Trito-Isaiah. In Isaiah 58:2, however, the verb *drš* ("to seek") is used in poetic parallelism with *ḥpṣ* ("to desire"). Isaiah 62:12, therefore, can be seen in direct parallelism with Isaiah 62:4. As "city not forsaken" is the direct antithesis of "forsaken," "sought out" or "desired" is synonymous with "I delight in her."

ISAIAH 63–64

Yhwh the Triumphant Champion: Isaiah 63:1-6

The brief hymn to Yhwh, the divine warrior who is victorious in the contest, contains for many modern readers some of the most troubling imagery in Trito-Isaiah, surpassed only perhaps by the grisly conclusion to the book. Yhwh is portrayed as coming in triumph, stained with the blood of his adversaries whom he has trampled underfoot. This brief passage is startling not only for its graphic imagery but also for its sudden and seemingly out-of-place appearance between the well-defined sections of Isaiah 60–62 and Isaiah 63:7–64:11. The former, which we have just looked at, highlighted the glorious restoration and transformation of Zion with imagery overflowing with light, wealth, and adornment. The latter, which we shall soon see, is a type of lament in which the people will implore Yhwh's favor to save them from their present distress brought on by their sins. The sharp contrast between this Divine Warrior hymn and its immediate surroundings has provided fuel for the line of argumentation against unity in Trito-Isaiah.[1]

Against this view that would see Isaiah 63:1-6 as totally isolated, Polan has argued for its close connection to Isaiah 60–62 and indeed its place within the structure and thought of Trito-Isaiah taken as a whole.[2] The first point to note is the significance in Trito-Isaiah of the verb *bwʾ* ("to come"). Trito-Isaiah begins with the announcement that Yhwh's

---

[1] Thus Westermann (*Isaiah 40–66*, 384) concludes: "Isaiah 63.1-6 cannot possibly, then, have been uttered either at the same time or by the same man as chs. 60–62." Blenkinsopp (*Isaiah 56–66*, 248) says of this passage: "It is clearly discontinuous with and from a different source than chs. 60–62."

[2] He graciously provided me with a copy of his unpublished paper: "The Divine Warrior Hymn of Isaiah 63:1-6: Its Structure and Function."

salvation will soon come (Isa 56:1). Isaiah 56–59 concludes on a similar note, stating, "And he will come to Zion as Redeemer" (Isa 59:20). Likewise, Isaiah 60–62 opens with the proclamation that Zion's light has come (Isa 60:1). It is not surprising, then, that this hymn in Isaiah 63:1-6 starts off with the question: "Who is this that comes from Edom?" (Isa 63:1). The coming that is described may be of a different type than the earlier oracles of salvation, but it is the flip side of the same coin—salvation for the righteous means the defeat of the forces of evil and oppression.[3]

In the second place is the close connection between this passage and the "peculiar" verse in the middle of Isaiah 60. That verse reads, "For the nation or kingdom / that will not serve you will perish / and the nations will be utterly destroyed" (Isa 60:12). We have already noted how many commentators do not quite know what to do with this harsh warning in the middle of an otherwise luminous chapter. As a consequence, it is often dismissed as a prosaic interpolation. Nevertheless, its central position and the theme of service to Zion situate it quite appropriately, both poetically and thematically, as the "main counter-message" of this chapter.[4] Looking beyond chapter 60 at the whole of Trito-Isaiah, one can also see how this seemingly anomalous verse belongs to the broader message of the prophet and indeed anticipates the Divine Warrior passage of Isaiah 63:1-6. The threat announced in Isaiah 60:12 is carried out in Isaiah 63:1-6.

Third, just on the other side of the Trito-Isaian core, we find yet another passage that is perhaps the most directly related to Isaiah 63:1-6 of all.[5] In discussing Isaiah 59:15b-20, some of the close connections between that passage and the present one were already raised. Isaiah 59:15b-20 is the portrait of Yhwh preparing for his act of vengeance upon his enemies, while Isaiah 63:1-6 is the picture of the victorious Yhwh returning from the contest. Each of these Trito-Isaian passages emphasizes Yhwh's garments (Isa 59:17; 63:1-3); Yhwh's solitary action, finding no one to help (Isa 59:16; 63:3, 5); the coming of Yhwh (Isa 59:20; 63:1); Yhwh's anger (Isa 59:18; 63:3, 5); victory (Isa 59:16-17; 63:5); and retribution (Isa 59:18; 63:4). In fact, if one were to remove the core of Isaiah 60–62 around which these passages stand (as well as the authorial window of Isa 59:21), the

---

[3] As Polan ("Divine Warrior") so aptly says: "It becomes clearer that the salvation announced at the beginning of Third Isaiah is not all glory and peace. We see that part of the salvific action of God is the destruction of injustice."

[4] Polan, "Zion, the Glory," 64–66.

[5] Even those who deny any connection to Isa 60–62 recognize the close similarities between this passage and Isa 59:15b-20. Together with those verses, Isa 63:1-6 is portrayed as a framing of Isa 60–62 by a later editor. See Koenen, "Ethik und Eschatologie," 84.

symmetry of the "bookends" surrounding the Trito-Isaian core can be clearly seen. Isaiah 59 concludes with the statement that Yhwh will come as redeemer to Zion. This promise is then immediately fulfilled in Isaiah 63:1 in which Yhwh is spotted coming from Edom.

It should be noted that although Yhwh (assuming the one responding to the questions—who is never named—is Yhwh) is described as coming in blood-stained garments from Edom, it does not necessarily follow that Edom is the object of his vengeance. In fact, Edom is not mentioned after the opening verse.[6] Rather, the expressed object of the divine anger is the rather generic and plural "peoples" (ʿmmym) of Isaiah 63:6. The region of Edom and Bozrah may simply be the location of the conflict described. Blenkinsopp has compared Isaiah 63:1-6 to Isaiah 34 where "the destruction of Edom takes place in the context of international and even cosmic disintegration and ruin."[7] The stunning similarities between Isaiah 34 and Isaiah 63:1-6 cannot be overlooked.[8] In both accounts, Edom is not the victim (or at least not the exclusive victim) of the divine violence but rather the location of a judgment against all peoples or nations. Both accounts also have graphic imagery emphasizing the extent of bloodshed. And both accounts make reference to the great slaughter of peoples as a "day of vengeance" (ywm nqm, Isa 34:8; 63:4). If anything, a more explicit judgment upon Edom is expressed in Isaiah 34:5 than anything found in Trito-Isaiah.

Another possibility, perhaps related to the aforementioned one, is that the desert to the south of Judah is simply the direction from which Yhwh traditionally marches.[9] The conglomeration of geographical indicators of the place from which Yhwh comes—Sinai, Seir, Edom, Teman, Mount Paran (see Deut 33:2; Judg 5:4; Ps 68:17; Hab 3:2)—all point to this southern region. The judgment "in Edom" rather than "of Edom"

---

[6] Isaiah 63:1 thus contains the only mention of a specific nation in Trito-Isaiah. This anomaly may have influenced attempts at emendation to eliminate the specific reference to Edom. Duhm (*Das Buch Jesaja*, 464) followed the suggestion of Lagarde to read *mēʾŏddām* ("red colored") for *mēʾĕdôm*.

[7] Blenkinsopp, *Isaiah 56–66*, 249.

[8] While noting differences between the passages, Blenkinsopp also points out what he sees as a closer similarity between Isa 34 and Isa 66:15-16, 22-24.

[9] This explanation is more fitting if one accepts the proposed reading of the participial root as ṣʿd ("walking" or "striding") following the Vulgate and Symmachus's Greek translation rather than MT's ṣʿh ("crouching" or "cowering"). The sense of MT is difficult to ascertain with the paradoxical combination of ṣʿh with khw ("his great might"). Perhaps it suggests a warrior's battle-ready stance, but again that appears out of place since this is a post-bellum scene. Polan ("Divine Warrior") understands the stooped figure of the victorious Yhwh as indicative of the scale of the battle and the fact that Yhwh has fought and conquered alone.

of Isaiah 63:1-6 thus is clearly Yhwh's judgment even if the Divine War-rior is not explicitly named in this passage. The play on words between Edom and blood (*dm*) and the play on meaning between Edom ("red") and the red-stained garments (Isa 63:2) also make a poetical case for Edom as the site of this blood-red judgment.

Returning to the question of the place and function of Isaiah 63:1-6 within the larger structure of Trito-Isaiah and the book of Isaiah, a few concluding observations may be made. Because of its distinctiveness and the abrupt transitions before and after this brief passage, it has been easy to isolate this text and to view it as rather discontinuous with what precedes and follows. Nevertheless, here it stands, a message of bloody judgment following the luminous proclamations of salvation and redemption in the Trito-Isaian core of chapters 60–62. We have already noted that this passage is not entirely unique either in the book of Isa-iah as a whole (with the antecedent in Isa 34) or in Trito-Isaiah (as it is anticipated by Isa 59:15b-20 and Isa 60:12, and anticipates the graphic conclusion of Isa 66:24). Looking at the more immediate context, the "darkness" of this passage is in many respects the mirror image of the "light" in preceding chapters.

Salvation/vindication is a two-edged sword in Isaiah. The vindica-tion of the righteous is at the same time retribution against the wicked. Here we strike at the core of Isaian and Trito-Isaian theology. The two ways—of the righteous and of the rebels—that we have seen throughout Trito-Isaiah is evidenced at its center as well. Where the light shines most brightly, shadows also appear. Thus, while the beginning of chapter 63 feels sudden and stark, it is about victory no less than chapters 60–62. As early as Isaiah 60:2 the darkness over the peoples (*ʿmmym*; compare with *ʾmmym* in Isa 63:6) contrasts with the dawning light of salvation for Yhwh's people. And in the center of that hymn of dawning salvation we noted the stern warning: "the nation or kingdom that will not serve you will perish" (Isa 60:12). What was threatened there is described as realized in Isaiah 63:1-6. Similarly in chapter 62, we were told that nations would see Zion's victory/vindication (Isa 62:2) and that this gain for Zion would be loss to her enemies and foreigners (Isa 62:8). So Isaiah 63:1-6 is not so out of place at all. The vindication promised in the preceding chapters is now presented as a *fait accompli*. Yhwh alone has won the victory for his people, but it is presented first of all as the defeat of his enemies.[10]

---

[10] One difference that has been noted between the parallel passages (Isa 59:15b-20 and Isa 63:1-6) on either side of Isa 60–62 is that the enemies in the former are those who have rebelled (*pšʿ*) against Yhwh (Isa 59:12-13)—the very citizens of Zion. The enemies in the latter are the nations and peoples (Isa 63:3, 6). Taken together the two

Having seen this passage's connections to the center of Trito-Isaiah in chapters 60 and 62, one final point needs to be made concerning its relation to chapter 61. At the very center of the multitiered chiastic structure of Trito-Isaiah is that famous prophetic call passage in which the prophet announces his divine commission "to proclaim a year of Yhwh's favor / and a day of vengeance for our God" (Isa 61:2). We noted how Isaiah 61:3 (like Isa 60:17) continues with a series of reversals expressed by word pairs set off by the term *tht* ("instead of").[11] The contrasting destinies expressed in these word pairs are set up by the contrast in the proclamation of "favor" (*rṣwn*) and "vengeance" (*nqm*). A very similar contrast is found in Isaiah 63:4: "A day of vengeance was in my heart / and the year of my redemption came." In both instances a year of Yhwh's action favoring or benefiting his people is paired with a day of Yhwh's action requiting his foes.[12] Once again, the two actions are but different facets of the one divine action of salvation/judgment.

Yhwh Our Father and Redeemer: Isaiah 63:7–64:11

The sudden shift to this new section, a psalm-like composition stretching into chapter 64, is likewise not without its logic. While many a form critic might note the parameters and the genre of these verses and assign them an independent *Sitz-im-Leben* quite distinct from the surrounding material, the content is intricately connected with the larger literary

---

passages remind us that just as salvation is not limited to Israel but open to foreigners who act rightly (Isa 56:3-7), so too vengeance against those who rebel does not discriminate according to nationality.

[11] One may also note the reversals expressed in Isa 60:18-20 with the phrase *lᵓ ᶜwd* ("no more").

[12] Muilenburg ("Book of Isaiah," 724) pointed to the language of "the acceptable year of the Lord and the day of vengeance" (Isa 61:2) as the main affinity between Isa 63:1-6 and Isa 60–62. Polan ("Divine Warrior") notes the inverted order of the phrases, with the day of vengeance in the second line of Isa 61:2 but in the first line of 63:4. He regards this as a distant chiasm, which would be fitting given Trito-Isaiah's ample use of chiastic structure. He also notes the different time periods involved, contrasting the shorter period of vengeance (a day) with the longer period of favor/redemption (a year). We need to consider, however, that "day of vengeance" may be a fixed phrase whose time period is not negotiable. On the other hand, this does seem theologically consonant with other biblical passages, such as Exod 20:5-6 and Ps 30:6. Finally, Willem Beuken (*Jesaja deel III A*, De predikning van het Oude Testament [Nijkerk: Callenbach, 1989], 202) has noted that the word pair *šnh/ywm* with both in the singular occurs only in Isa 34:8; 61:2; and 63:4.

context.[13] Just as we heard an account of the defeat of Yhwh's enemies in the gory judgment of Isaiah 63:1-6, now the prophet recounts Yhwh's gracious acts (*ḥsdy yhwh*) on behalf of his people. The disconnect, if there is one, is that the redemption and victory recounted are now events in the distant past, and Yhwh's "year of redemption" (which came in Isa 63:4) has in fact not yet arrived. In spite of the optimistic introduction in Isaiah 63:7, the mood shifts to a more penitent rather than triumphant character as the prophetic psalmist's reflections move from the past to the present. The people are still on the wrong side of Yhwh's righteousness and are treated as his enemy against whom he wars (Isa 63:10), putting them on the side of the peoples of Isaiah 63:6.

The logic behind this section of text and its place within Trito-Isaiah can perhaps best be understood in terms of the tension between prophetic pronouncement and fulfillment. Throughout Trito-Isaiah we are told that Yhwh's salvation and victory are coming. With regard to this constant theme, the image of the dawning light is in many ways the most significant. It has appeared and is visible to us now, but it has not yet reached its full measure. It is in this tension between the already and the not yet that the focus and mood of Isaiah 63:7–64:11 shifts back to the "not yet" immediately after Isaiah 63:1-6 had seemingly announced Yhwh's arrival and triumph. But note that even in that passage, Yhwh is coming from Edom; he has not yet arrived in Zion. His defeat of the peoples can be seen as the first step toward the deliverance and glorification of Zion. But the pace of progress is perhaps not what was expected. The setbacks and delays are greater than anticipated. Questions and doubts begin to impinge on hope, and so the prophet gives words to the people as they lament their present condition and implore Yhwh for a dramatic intervention into the current state of affairs.

Many have noted the similarities between Isaiah 63:7–64:11 and communal psalms of lament.[14] Form critics, beginning with Hermann Gunkel, have defined the main divisions within this category of psalm: (1) address to Yhwh, (2) lament over misfortune (usually political in nature), (3) petition to Yhwh to change misfortune, (4) expression of confidence (often replaced by an appeal to Yhwh to continue to act as in the past), and (5) vow of praise anticipating a positive response.[15] This passage

---

[13] Blenkinsopp (*Isaiah 56–66*, 257) notes how the questions at the end of this section (Isa 64:11) connect it to the response (of sorts) that one finds in Isa 65:1-12. He sees, however, no connection between this section and the preceding Divine Warrior hymn.

[14] Richard Bautch, "Lament Regained in Trito-Isaiah's Penitential Prayer," in *Seeking the Favor of God*, vol. 1: *The Origins of Penitential Prayer in Second Temple Judaism* (Atlanta: Society of Biblical Literature, 2006), 83–99.

[15] Hermann Gunkel, *Einleitung in die Psalmen*, ed. J. Bergrich (Göttingen: Vandenhoeck & Ruprecht, 1933), 125.

in Isaiah shows signs of all of these elements with the exception of the last. Although the passage does not begin with an invocation of Yhwh or God (such as Pss 12 and 44, e.g.), the vocative is used for Yhwh in Isaiah 63:16-17 and 64:7-8, 11. The lament is clearly associated with the ruin of the temple in Isaiah 63:18 and 64:9-10.[16] Petition is made to Yhwh to change the people's fortune in Isaiah 63:15 and 64:8. The largest part of this Isaian psalm is the recollection of past actions (Isa 63:7-9, 11-14; 64:2-3) and an appeal to Yhwh to renew them (Isa 63:15-17; 63:19b–64:1; 64:8).

Instead of concluding with a confident expression of trust in God (see Pss 12:7; 79:13), the Isaian psalm ends with a question rather than a statement. There is a sense of drama and unrelieved tension in this passage from Isaiah, where we can feel the desperate situation of Israel as they implore Yhwh for aid.[17] One might argue that the answer to the rhetorical question with which the passage ends—"Will you keep silent and afflict us so greatly?"—is "no" but the weight of that hanging question speaks to the gravity of the situation and the unclear outcome at the time the words are spoken.

Looking more closely at the content and imagery of this passage, one notes first of all its opening theme in Isaiah 63:7: "I will recall the mercies of Yhwh" (*ḥsdy yhwh 'zkyr*). The introit, similar to that of Psalm 89, once again reminds us of the Davidic covenant.[18] Both texts celebrate God's deeds and promises of the past while asking where God's presence is now. One slight variation between the texts is that in Psalm 89 the faithful love of Yhwh was sung, whereas here in Isaiah it is remembered. Memory plays a key role for Trito-Isaiah, as it obviously does more generally for the Jewish and Christian religions. We just read in the previous chapter of the watchmen on Jerusalem's walls who are to take no rest and give Yhwh no rest as they remind him of what he must do for Jerusalem. These sentinels, in fact, were called the "remembrancers" of Yhwh (Isa 62:6).[19] The plural participle *mzkrym* of Isaiah 62:6 is of the same verb

---

[16] In this respect Isa 63:7–64:11 is very similar to Pss 74 and 79, which also lament the ruin of Jerusalem and the temple, asking how long before Yhwh will act on his people's behalf.

[17] In this it is not as distinct from the communal psalms of lament as some might argue. Psalm 44, for example, ends with a similar questioning and plea, asking when Yhwh will act and imploring him to do so.

[18] Nurmela (*Mouth of the Lord*, 122) notes that the expression *ḥsdy yhwh* occurs but four times in the Bible, the other two being Ps 107:43 and Lam 3:22. All four instances are in contexts of extreme adversity. Lamentations and Ps 89 are both clearly post-destruction texts like Isa 63:7–64:11. Psalm 107 is more generic, speaking about God's saving action from several types of adversity.

[19] Translated quite literally thus in the NJPS.

(*zkr*) with which the prophet begins his psalm here, perhaps deliberately identifying himself as such a *mzkr*.

The verb *zkr* will show up again in verse 11 in one of the most difficult passages of Trito-Isaiah. The first half of this verse quite literally reads, "Then he remembered the days of old, Moses his people." Many would understand the subject of the verb "to remember" as the people.[20] But it is also possible to see the subject as Yhwh, who is also the subject of the masculine singular verbs in verse 10.[21] This understanding would fit in well with the earlier exhortations to the watchmen to "remind Yhwh" in Isaiah 62:6. Isaiah 63:11 would then be the successful result of the day and night supplications of the *mzkrym*. Yhwh has remembered the days of old and his promises to Moses and his people from the time of the Exodus. Alternatively, if it is the people who are remembering the days of old, then this is the first step in their turning back to Yhwh and away from their rebellious ways (Isa 63:10). Taken either way, memory plays a key role in the ultimate revival and restoration of Zion and its inhabitants.

After its introductory verse, this Isaian psalm continues in an unusually historical vein for Trito-Isaiah, recalling Moses and the exodus (Isa 63:11-14), Abraham (Isa 63:16), and Israel (Isa 63:16). In general, one might say that Trito-Isaiah is usually more future oriented, looking forward to the vindication of Jerusalem and the new age to come that is most poignantly expressed in the language of "a new heaven and a new earth" (Isa 65:17). But that glorious future is grounded in the promises of the past, and it is fitting (given Trito-Isaiah's repeated use of the verb *zkr*) that some recital of those glorious deeds of old and mention of Israel's ancestors be included in these chapters.

Another theme that carries over from Isaiah 63:1-6 is the idea of Yhwh alone as the savior of his people. Isaiah 63:3 spoke of Yhwh who trod out the vintage alone (*lbdy*) having no one with him. Likewise, Isaiah 63:5 reasserted that Yhwh had no help or assistance but triumphed through his own strength (*zrʿy*) and fury (*ḥmty*).[22] Now in Isaiah 63:8b-9 a similar

---

[20] Thus, Paul (*Isaiah 40–66*, 573) suggests emending the vocalization of MT to the plural form *vayyizkĕru*. Blenkinsopp (*Isaiah 56–66*, 254), noting that MT and all ancient versions have the singular, offers that the singular form can refer to either Yhwh or the people (as a collective) and that the latter makes more sense. Similarly, Whybray (*Isaiah 40–66*, 258) claims that "the subject is clearly the people of Israel, though it is probably not necessary to emend the verb to the plural as is proposed by some commentators."

[21] So Childs (*Isaiah*, 524). Less likely is the attempt to understand Moses as the subject rather than the object of the verb.

[22] A somewhat related concept with regard to this "solitude" of Yhwh is found in Deutero-Isaiah (Isa 42:8; 45:5-6, 14, 18, 21-22; 46:9). In those passages, however, the

sentiment is expressed, although the passage is controversial due to the difference between the Kethib and the Qere. The consonantal text (Kethib), which is also reflected in LXX, reads, "So he became their savior in all their afflictions. It was not an angel or a messenger; his presence saved them." The vocalization of MT (Qere) gives, "So he became their savior. In all their afflictions he was afflicted. And the angel of his presence saved them." While the Kethib more clearly highlights the idea of Yhwh acting alone, it must be pointed out that the Qere (while perhaps not as obviously) does so as well. For the "angel of his presence" (*ml˒k pnyw*) is not some being other than Yhwh but an extension of Yhwh himself.[23] In the end, whichever way one chooses to read this passage, the point is that Yhwh alone was their savior, and "He himself redeemed them" (*hw˒ g˒lm*, Isa 63:9b).[24]

In the middle of verse 14 the voice and tenor of the passage suddenly changes from a remembering of the kind acts (*ḥsdy yhwh*) of Yhwh in the past (speaking about Yhwh in the third person) to a direct address to Yhwh. Now speaking to Yhwh in the second person, Trito-Isaiah implores Yhwh to intervene and act on behalf of his people in some of the most stirring language and imagery in all of Scripture. The shift from past to present reveals a sharp contrast between then and now. The wonders of Yhwh's actions in Israel's history are not immediately evident now to Trito-Isaiah. The questioning that began in the third person in verse 11 ("Where is the one who brought them up from the sea?") continues from verse 15 onward as direct speech to Yhwh ("Where is your zeal and your might?").

Beginning with Isaiah 63:16 there are three distinct statements identifying and claiming Yhwh as "father":

---

idea is that Yhwh is God alone; there is no other god beside him. Isa 63:3 emphasizes Yhwh's solitude in acting without any human assistance. Isa 63:5 is generic and ambiguous ("no help"). Following verse 3 this is generally taken to mean no human help, but it could refer to heavenly beings as well.

[23] The Qere would match up more closely with the passages in Deutero-Isaiah, emphasizing Yhwh as the only divine agent. The Kethib would add a new dimension to the "solitude" of Yhwh in Isaiah. Having no gods (Deutero-Isaiah) and no humans (Isa 63:3) with him, Isa 63:8b-9 would now add the idea of no intermediaries as well.

[24] The emphatic pronoun in the second half of verse 9 reemphasizes Yhwh as the sole agent in question. My own preference is for the reading of the Kethib and LXX, which is also reflected in 1QIsa[a] with the plene spelling of the negative particle (*lw˒*) instead of the preposition with suffix.

Isaiah 63:16a	*ky ᵓth ᵓbynw*	Surely you are our father.
Isaiah 63:16b	*ᵓth yhwh ᵓbynw*	You, Yhwh, are our father.
Isaiah 64:7a	*wᶜth yhwh ᵓbynw ᵓth*	But now, Yhwh, our father are you.

The threefold repetition is stunning, especially when one considers the infrequency with which Yhwh is addressed as "father" in the Hebrew Scriptures. The triple usage of words, so frequently employed in Trito-Isaiah, imparts a profound emphasis to the dramatic claim. Even when one considers the few other passages where God is called father, it is almost invariably in the form of a question or a hypothetical statement. "Is not he your father, who created you?" (Deut 32:6); "Have you not just now called to me, 'my Father'?" (Jer 3:4); "And I thought you would call me, my Father" (Jer 3:19); "If then I am a father, where is the honor due me?" (Mal 1:6); "Have we not all one father? Has not one God created us?" (Mal 2:10).[25] The Isaian passages stand in stark contrast to these other formulations by their emphasis and brevity, three times combining the second-person singular pronoun with "our father."

We may also note how the statements build throughout the passage. The first occurrence in Isaiah 63:16a simply juxtaposes the pronoun and suffixed noun: "you [are] our father." The second in Isaiah 63:16b adds the divine name in the vocative between these elements: "you, Yhwh, [are] our father." The third occurrence, at a distance from the first two, reverses the order of the key terms "you" and "our father" (another example of distant chiasm in Trito-Isaiah). Furthermore, it adds even more emphasis to what has been emphasized throughout—the direct address to Yhwh as "you" in claiming him as father. This is accomplished by another layer of chiasm. The line is arranged so the pronoun falls at the end. The emphasis given the pronoun "you" (*ᵓth*) is amplified by the pun with the word "now" (*ᶜth*) placed at the beginning of the line. Perhaps the best way to render this wordplay in translation would be through adding emphasis: "But now, Yhwh, YOU are our father."

A further point to note is the presence of secondary metaphors associated with the primary metaphor of "father" in these verses. Isaiah 63:16 identifies Yhwh as the people's redeemer (*gᵓl*) as well as their father. Similarly, Isaiah 64:7 speaks of Yhwh as both father and potter (*yṣr*). These parallel metaphors help to elucidate precisely what is intended by Trito-Isaiah's direct address to Yhwh as father.

---

[25] Examples taken from Niskanen, "Yhwh as Father," 398.

The first pairing—father and redeemer—highlights the covenantal bond between Yhwh and Israel understood as a bond of kinship.[26] This can be seen especially in light of the two statements sandwiched between the dual claims of Yhwh's fatherhood in Isaiah 63:16: "For Abraham does not know us, and Israel does not acknowledge us." The human ancestors (fathers) of the Israelites do not or will not claim paternity for their rebellious children. This is no matter to Trito-Isaiah as a higher appeal is made to Yhwh as the true tribal head or father of the Israelites. The previous allusions to the Exodus (Isa 63:11-13) and coming allusions to Sinai (Isa 63:19–64:2) suddenly come into clearer focus. The father-son relationship created by the exodus event and Sinai covenant (see Exod 4:22; Hos 11:1) is the foundation for Trito-Isaiah's emotional appeal to Yhwh as father. Calling Yhwh "our redeemer from of old" (*g'lnw m'wlm*) further points to these ancient events whereby Yhwh became their avenging kinsman. It also appeals to Yhwh's duty and responsibility to Israel in their covenant relationship. As their redeemer/avenger (*g'l*), Yhwh is bound to act on their behalf as Israel's kin.

The second pairing—father and potter—both reinforces and balances the claims made by the father-redeemer analogy. On the one hand, the potter image speaks of making or creating. But this is no universal creation to which Trito-Isaiah alludes, but rather the creation of Yhwh's people Israel. While it may be tempting to see the reference to Yhwh as potter (*yṣr*) as primarily an allusion to Genesis 2:7 where Yhwh God forms (*yṣr*) *adam* out of the earth, the context in Isaiah 64 continually refers not to humanity in general but to the Israelites and Zion. The potter metaphor, combined with that of father in Isaiah 64:7, thus is a reference to the making and begetting of Israel by Yhwh. The same idea is expressed in Deuteronomy 32:6: "Is he not your father who created you, who made you and established you?" There, the father metaphor is used in conjunction with the verbs "create" (*qnh*), "make" (*'śh*), and "establish" (*knn*)—all referring specifically to Israel. So on the one hand, the father-potter pairing reinforces the father-redeemer analogy, which

---

[26] Ibid., 401. F. Charles Fensham ("Father and Son as Terminology for Treaty and Covenant," in *Near Eastern Studies in Honor of W. F. Albright*, ed. H. Goedicke [Baltimore: Johns Hopkins University Press, 1971], 121–35) identified the father metaphor as an original part of the idea of covenant in ancient Near Eastern texts. The addition here of the term *g'l* (which may be variously translated as "redeemer," "avenger," or "next of kin") reinforces the covenant/kinship expressed by the term "father." As Frank Moore Cross Jr. (*From Epic to Canon: History and Literature in Ancient Israel* [Baltimore: Johns Hopkins University Press, 2000], 3–21) has also pointed out, the language of kinship is the language of covenant because a covenant is essentially a type of "kinship in law."

emphasizes Yhwh's unique relationship to Israel and hence his covenantal obligation to them.

On the other hand, the potter imagery has a strong precedent, especially in the book of Jeremiah, of which Trito-Isaiah is certainly aware.[27]
Jeremiah's visit to the potter's house in Jeremiah 18:1-10 highlights the
complete freedom that the potter (Yhwh) has in shaping the clay (Israel).
Here the potter owes the clay nothing and is free to fashion it—to create
or destroy—at will. This point is repeated in Deutero-Isaiah, where it
takes up the potter metaphor in Isaiah 45:9-11 (in conjunction with both
father and mother metaphors). The complete freedom and inscrutability of Yhwh as the "potter" of Israel is underscored.[28] This freedom of
the potter in Isaiah 64:7 serves to balance the obligation of the redeemer
in Isaiah 63:16. The prophet stresses the unworthiness of the people to
receive any assistance from Yhwh in the verses leading up to the father-
potter imagery (Isa 64:4-6). Due nothing and deserving of nothing, the
people's pleas to Yhwh, father and potter, to look down and intervene
on their behalf take on a pathetically desperate tone.

The concluding verses of Isaiah 64 make one final appeal to Yhwh.
Reaching beyond what Yhwh might owe them or what they might merit,
Trito-Isaiah calls on Yhwh to look on "your holy cities," "Zion," "Jerusalem," and "our holy and beautiful house" (Isa 64:9-10). First of all, the
inclusion of "your holy cities" (*ʿry qdšk*) in this constellation of familiar
Isaian points of reference is a bit unusual. The phrase is used nowhere
else in the Bible, and the Trito-Isaian scope up to this point has been
focused up close on Jerusalem/Zion alone.[29] The appeal now, in conjunction with the potter metaphor, is for Yhwh to consider his work that has
been destroyed, thus including the Judean cities beyond Jerusalem. The
references to Zion and Jerusalem becoming a desert and a desolation are
typical enough. One of the main foci of Trito-Isaiah is the restoration of
desolate Zion, as we have seen. There is, however, one final expression
used here that requires some analysis due to its peculiar nature.

In verse 10, Trito-Isaiah speaks of the destruction of "our holy and
beautiful house" (*byt qdšnw wtpʾrtnw*). This expression is unparalleled

---

[27] The dependence of the father metaphor in Isa 63–64 on Jer 3 and 31 has also been
noted. See Johannes Goldstein, *Das Gebet der Gottesknechte*, WMANT 92 (Neukirchen-
Vluyn: Neukirchener Verlag, 2001), 245–46.

[28] Isaiah 45:12 goes on to speak of a more universal creative activity of God, but Isa
45:9-11, like Isa 64:7, is speaking of the creation, forming, and birth of Israel.

[29] Although the exact phrase is found nowhere else, post-destruction literature
does frequently speak of the destruction of other sites in conjunction with Jerusalem
by using other language (e.g., Lam 2:2-5, which refers to the destruction of the "for-
tresses" [*mbṣrym*] and "palaces" [*ʾrmnwt*] of Judah and Israel).

anywhere in the biblical text. The former splendor (*tp'rt*) of the now-destroyed temple recalls the imagery of shining light and glory from the Trito-Isaian core of chapters 60–62. That the temple is included in this communal lament over Jerusalem is not unusual at all. The temple has figured prominently from the opening chapter of Trito-Isaiah. What is most unusual about this passage, however, is the first common plural possessive suffixes. What was called "your holy place" (*qdšk*) in Isaiah 63:18 is now "our holy place" (*qdšnw*). This is especially unusual in light of the fact that the prophet has been highlighting Yhwh's ownership of both people (Isa 64:8) and cities (Isa 64:9) under the potter imagery. The rhetorical appeal up to this point has been: "Act on behalf of what you have made and what belongs to you!" But now the prophet, speaking on behalf of the people, claims ownership of the temple and mourns what the people have lost: "All that was precious to us is ruined" (Isa 64:10b).[30]

What began in verse 9 to look like a typical appeal to Yhwh to act in his own interest—to protect his property, to guard his honor, to look after his sanctuary—takes a turn in verse 10, becoming a plea to have pity on a people's misery. The emotive appeal here is at its most profound (and the style and tone most akin to the communal psalms of lament and the book of Lamentations). Having witnessed the people lose everything (indeed, the only thing!) they hold dear, who cannot be moved to compassion? To compound the situation, that which they have lost is the very temple "where our fathers praised you" (Isa 64:10ab). If the tragedy of the people's losing their most precious possession is not enough to stir Yhwh to action, the prophet adds that what they cherished most was their very relationship with Yhwh. The prophet has made his case and casts down the concluding challenge to Yhwh. "Considering these things, will you restrain yourself, Yhwh? Will you remain silent and afflict us so greatly?" (Isa 64:11).[31]

---

[30] Reading the singular *mḥmdnw* as a singular (referring to the temple) rather than the plural *mḥmdynw* of MT. See BHS which cites many manuscripts, the Syriac, Targums, Arabic, and Ethiopic in support of this reading. The poetic parallelism of the verse also indicates the singular temple as referent, and the singular verb would seem to require this understanding.

[31] The emotionally charged questions that conclude the passage in Isaiah are once more reminiscent of Ps 89 in its ending (Ps 89:47-52), pleading with a merciful and faithful Yhwh to act on behalf of his suffering servants.

ISAIAH 65

Heightened Judgment: Isaiah 65:1-16

Yhwh's response to the rhetorically powerful pleading of Isaiah 63:7–64:11 comes immediately, but it would not appear to be the answer hoped for by the actual or rhetorical questions with which the preceding chapter concludes. In this it is very similar to the response of Yhwh in the book of Job (Job 38–41). Neither questioner receives what he expects, and in both cases the ones who ask are taken to task as Yhwh disabuses them of their perceived right and forces them to view reality in a new light from the divine perspective. The requested divine intervention neither happens nor is promised in Trito-Isaiah (although a different type of divine response will be announced in verse 6). Rather, Yhwh responds that he has been responding all along. He has been answering those who would not ask and trying to be found by those who would not seek. The unusual *Niphal* stem for the verbs *drš* and *mṣʾ* in Isaiah 65:1 is best understood in the tolerative sense. Hence, "I allowed myself to be asked" is the equivalent of "I answered" and "I allowed myself to be found."[1] In his eagerness to encounter his people, Yhwh allows for a role reversal, responding in words more typical of the prophet who is called by crying out: "Here I am!" (see Isa 6:8).

Some commentators, following Duhm, would doubt that this chapter actually contains a response to the concluding questions of the previous.[2] As Childs points out, this may be due to the predominance of a form-critical approach that tends toward fragmentation of the literature.[3]

---

[1] See Joüon and Muraoka, *Grammar of Biblical Hebrew*, 139.

[2] See, e.g., Whybray, *Isaiah 40–66*, 266; Blenkinsopp, *Isaiah 56–66*, 268; Westermann, *Isaiah 40–66*, 398–402.

[3] Childs, *Isaiah*, 532–33.

Duhm, however, has made a valid point in that those addressed in Isaiah 65:1-7 bear little similarity to the penitent community pleading with Yhwh in Isaiah 63:7–64:11. The commonality they share is their sinfulness, but while the first group acknowledges this (Isa 64:4-6), the second appears utterly blind to it (Isa 65:5). While there may in all likelihood have been originally disparate settings and addressees of these passages, we cannot ignore their current placement in the present text. One can be a form critic and still appreciate the richness and interplay in the completed literary composition. As Hanson states: "As a separate unit, chapter 65 was originally written as a highly polemical salvation-judgment oracle. . . . Once it was placed after the lament, however, it came to serve an added purpose, namely, to provide an answer to the questions and complaints of the lament."[4]

Another indication of continuity between chapters 64 and 65 can be found in Isaiah 65:6. When Yhwh says that he will not be silent (*ḥšh*), this is another sign that this chapter is indeed a response to the concluding plea of chapter 64. The final verse there asked of Yhwh if he would remain silent (*ḥšh*). This theme of not keeping silent also recalls the opening verse of chapter 62, where the speaker vows not to be silent. While most commentators understand those words as belonging specifically to the prophetic herald and not to Yhwh, it was also noted that the Septuagint appears to understand them as the voice of God, since it substitutes first-person possessive pronouns in the latter half of the verse for the third-person forms found in MT. In any event, the silence of Yhwh has been a running thread through Trito- (and Deutero-) Isaiah (Isa 42:14; 57:11; 64:11).[5] Whether 62:1 signals a change in Yhwh's stance or represents the prophetic pestering (as in the task of the sentinels a few verses later in Isa 62:6-7) that provokes Yhwh to action, that moment of divine intervention is clearly stated in the voice of Yhwh in Isaiah 65:6. The prophetic appeals begun in chapter 62 and building through the lament of chapters 63–64 finally achieve their purpose of spurring divine activity and Yhwh's promise of full retribution here.

A final point in favor of a continuous reading from chapter 64 through 65 is that the contrast made between the people of Isaiah 63:7–64:11 and Isaiah 65 is not as clear cut as often supposed. First of all, if one broadens the horizon and speaks of Isaiah 65 *in toto* as a unit, it may be observed that not only the wicked and the rebels but also the servants of Yhwh come into play (Isa 65:8-9, 13-15). While some may claim that this "religiously divided community" is not to be found in Isaiah 63:7–64:11, there are

---

[4] Hanson, *Isaiah 40–66*, 241.
[5] As Blenkinsopp (*Isaiah 56–66*, 233) points out, this idea of the silence of God is also found more broadly in post-destruction literature (e.g., Ps 28:1; 83:2).

indications in that Isaiah psalm pointing to both the righteous (Isa 63:8, 11, 18; 64:5) and the wicked (Isa 63:10; 64:5-7).[6] It may be argued that in Isaiah 63:7–64:11 the righteous and wicked are in fact one and the same people at different moments, whereas in Isaiah 65 they constitute different people at the same moment. This is a fair observation, but we must add to it a consideration of the dramatic movement as we approach the climax and conclusion of Trito-Isaiah and the book of Isaiah. The lament of Isaiah 63–64 pointed to a historical pattern of rebellion and return. The people of Israel—oscillating between holiness and sin—are now coming, in the thought of Trito-Isaiah, to a day of reckoning. The time for fence sitting or shifting allegiances is rapidly coming to an end, and the eschatological judgment and final parting of the ways is about to be revealed.

The teaching of the two ways that has been so prominent throughout the book of Isaiah in general and Trito-Isaiah in particular reaches its climax in the penultimate chapter of both. The rapid back-and-forth motion and the odd juxtaposition of passages of salvation and judgment in Isaiah 56–66 are found in microcosm in Isaiah 65. We can divide the chapter as follows:

Condemnation of Rebels		Salvation for Yhwh's Servants
Isa 65:1-7		Isa 65:8-10
Isa 65:11-12		
	Isa 65:13-16	
		Isa 65:17-25
Isa 65:25b		

The more leisurely unfolding contrast in the first twelve verses accelerates into a rapid-fire back-and-forth in verses 13-16. This broadens out once more into the eschatological vision of salvation in verses 17-25, but not without a final metaphor of judgment in the final verse.

At the very start of this chapter contrasting these two ways, a double contrast is made by Trito-Isaiah. First, we see the contrast between the speaker of Isaiah 65:1-7—identified as Yhwh in Isaiah 65:7—and the people

[6] Whybray (*Isaiah 56–66*, 266) is adamant in arguing for "no connexion between the two passages." Paul (*Isaiah 40–66*, 589), on the other hand, claims that "the chapter is connected to the previous unit by multiple terms and expressions."

who are addressed. Before we even begin to address the ways of the righteous and the wicked we must consider the ways of Yhwh versus those of humans. Back in the chapter on the cusp between Second and Third Isaiah, this contrast had already been drawn (Isa 55:8-9). There, the mercy and forgiveness of a God who wants to be sought was brought into relief (Isa 55:6-7). Here too in Isaiah 65, Yhwh is the picture of grace and long suffering in his solicitude for the people; they, on the other hand, are disinterested, disloyal, and utterly self-centered. He calls out to the people even though they will not call on him. He makes every effort to be found, but they will not seek. He continues to extend his hands to the people even when this gesture is met with indifference and disdain. This initial contrast in Isaiah 65:1-5 concludes with the pronouncement of judgment in Isaiah 65:6-7.

A second contrast unfolds in the following verses. Not all of the people have rebelled and strayed, but the remnant, identified as Yhwh's servants, is introduced in Isaiah 65:8-10. Unlike the first group, these do seek Yhwh (Isa 65:10) and so will be blessed with the inheritance of hills and valleys for them and their flocks. The blessing of inheriting Yhwh's mountain (Isa 65:9) by the servants contrasts with the judgment pronounced once more on the wicked precisely because they forget Yhwh's holy mountain (Isa 65:11). The temple figures prominently in this judgment passage, both as the criterion by which judgment is made (concern for seeking Yhwh in his holy place) and as the blessing bestowed on those who meet this criterion (being allowed to dwell on God's mountain). Once again we see the tight *contrapasso* of Isaiah whereby, not only are the wicked fittingly punished, but the righteous are also oppositely rewarded. Just as throughout Trito-Isaiah *ṣdqh* understood as righteous action leads to *ṣdqh* understood as victory or deliverance, so also seeking Yhwh on his holy mountain (*ṣdqh* in the former sense) leads to being with Yhwh on his holy mountain (*ṣdqh* in the latter sense).

The way that is not good in which the people walk is characterized in Isaiah 65:3-4 by cultic and dietary transgressions. This is a bit unusual in the book of Isaiah, although the locations of the sacrifices mentioned may be given to indicate worship of deities other than Yhwh. These may be mentioned explicitly in verse 11, which describes the preparation of offerings for Gad ("good fortune" or "luck") and Meni ("fortune" or "destiny"). Thus, the mention of eating of pork and other unclean items may be focused primarily on idolatrous sacrifices rather than kashrut violations. The locations of gardens, tombs, and secret places, along with the mountains and hills in verse 7, may also intentionally contrast with Yhwh's holy mountain and the prominence of the Jerusalem temple for Isaiah. The parody on holiness in verse 5 would also fit into this picture in which Trito-Isaiah understands the true locus of holiness to be Yhwh's mountain (Isa 65:11). The thrust of Isaiah 65:1-7 is the utter rejection and disdain shown to Yhwh by the people. The comment in verse 7 that the people insult or taunt (*ḥrp*) Yhwh by these sacrificial and dietary actions further supports the argument that the core offense in question is indeed idolatry.

All is not lost, however, for the Isaian remnant resurfaces in verses 8-9 under the image of juice or new wine (*tyrwš*) that remains in a bunch of grapes. Reading back through the book of Isaiah, one recalls first of all the gruesome imagery of crushed grapes encountered in the Divine Warrior hymn of Isaiah 63:1-6. In contrast to the present text, which recounts the proverb "do not destroy it for a blessing is in it," the earlier Trito-Isaian passage recounts the pressing of these grapes as a violent act of destruction. The juice in them was not described as being made into the blessing of wine (see Ps 104:15; Eccl 10:19; Sir 31:37) but rather construed as the blood of Yhwh's enemies being squeezed out of them. Isaiah 65:8, by way of contrast, points to Yhwh's benevolent action on behalf of his servants so that he will not destroy "the whole" (*hkl*).

Reaching even further back into the book of Isaiah, one happens upon the famous vineyard song of Isaiah 5. The emphasis there was on the utter worthlessness of the crop of wild grapes, which represented the inhabitants of Jerusalem and Judah. Once again we note a contrast between the former imagery and the present; what was an image of judgment has become an image of salvation for a remnant. The idea that there is something worth saving, however, is certainly not new in Isaiah. The remnant that is saved is a major Isaian theme from the book's earliest chapters. In Isaiah 1:9 the prophet mentions a few survivors (*śrd*), Isaiah 1:27 promises salvation for the repentant (*šwb*), and Isaiah 4:2-3 speaks of both those who escape (*plṭ*) and the remnant in Zion (*š'r*). The novelty in Trito-Isaiah is that this remnant is now identified as the Trito-Isaian "servants" and that the imagery of grapes and wine has been transformed from language of judgment to that of salvation.

The blessings of salvation for the servants are further expressed in verse 9 in the language of descendants, inheritance, and possession. There is an intensifying progressive parallelism in this verse. First comes the promise of offspring, literally "seed" (*zr'*), emphasizing biological life and generation. Next the prophet mentions heirs (*yrš*) who, while being the same as the seed inasmuch as they are children of the parents, are also something more in their social and legal status. In the third place, Yhwh calls them his chosen ones (*bḥr*), a status that rises above that derived from natural generation by Yhwh's gracious election. And, finally, they are called "my servants," the fullest expression for the righteous in Trito-Isaiah as Yhwh's call meets with a full human response.[7] Similarly, there

---

[7] The designations "chosen" and "servants," linked here by poetic parallelism, are also closely connected in Deutero-Isaiah, as has been noted by various commentators (e.g., Westermann, *Isaiah 40–66*, 404; Scullion, *Isaiah 40–66*, 201).

is a verbal movement from being brought forth, to inheriting, to dwell-ing. The final situation described—dwelling on Yhwh's mountain(s)—is nothing less than a paradisiacal state in Isaian theology.

After the brief interlude of this beatific vision, the contrast with the wicked returns in verses 11-12. The sharpness of the contrast drawn between the two camps in this chapter has been noted by several com-mentators.[8] We have pointed out the significance of "remembering" in Trito-Isaiah. Now we see that the wicked are characterized by the op-posite trait. They not only forsake (*ʿzb*) Yhwh but also forget (*škḥ*) his holy mountain. The antitheses between those who abandon Yhwh and the servants continue in verse 12, which also contrasts the actions of the wicked with the action of Yhwh himself. Yhwh brings the accusation against them that when he called they did not answer. This is the direct opposite of what is described in Isaiah 65:1 where Yhwh responded to a people who did not ask. The people's choosing what Yhwh does not desire is also the antithesis of the eunuchs' actions mentioned at the very beginning of Trito-Isaiah. They were acceptable precisely because they had chosen what Yhwh desires (Isa 56:4).

The contrast between the two ways here in Isaiah 65 reaches its own climax in verses 13-15 where the fates of the servants of Yhwh and those addressed who have not sought him are expressed in five sets of polar opposites.

My Servants	You (pl.)
will eat	will hunger
will drink	will thirst
will rejoice	will be put to shame
will shout for joy of heart	will cry out for anguish of heart
will be given a different name	will leave your name as a curse for my chosen

The future state of each group, presented in antithetical fashion, is both reminiscent of the descriptions of future blessings and curses found in Deuteronomy 28 and anticipatory of the gospel beatitudes, especially

---

[8] E.g., Childs, *Isaiah*, 537; Blenkinsopp (*Isaiah 56–66*, 273) even subtitles Isa 65:8-12 as "Who Are and Are Not God's People."

in their Lucan form.[9] There is a chiastic reversal in the final pair in verse 15, whereby the entire series begins and ends on a positive note of the blessings for the servants of Yhwh. The new name given to the servants is the harbinger of the renewal of all creation that will be announced in Isaiah 65:17.[10] This scene of judgment and division in verses 13-15 is the necessary prelude to a future idyllic state in which "the former troubles will be forgotten" (Isa 65:16). The concept of remembering/forgetting occurs once more here, but this time forgetting is the proper course to take with regard to the distress of the past (which is, in fact, the present moment of distress for Trito-Isaiah).

The Isaian Utopia: Isaiah 65:17-25

The imminent future that is so frequently the temporal focus of Trito-Isaiah is expressed in Isaiah 65:17 with the common construction of the particle *hnnh* followed by the active participle: "See, I am about to create." There is a strong similarity here to the passage in Deutero-Isaiah that calls for the forgetting of things in the past in order to perceive God's pending action in the world (Isa 43:18-19). The language of a new heaven and a new earth along with the following idyllic imagery of commonplace centenarians and herbivorous lions easily lends itself to eschatological readings.[11] One should not, however, allow the hyperbolic and mytho-poetic language to mislead one into thinking Trito-Isaiah is referring to some divine act that brings human history to a close or that he is relocating salvation outside of history. Whatever the value of allegorical, typological, and eschatological interpretations of this passage, there remains beneath them the historical sense by which Trito-Isaiah refers to the transformation of Jerusalem by the hand of Yhwh entering precisely at this moment into history.

---

[9] Blenkinsopp (*Isaiah 56–66*, 281) especially highlights the close parallel with the language of the curse in Deut 28:47, but one can say that that entire chapter with its antithetical blessings and curses provides a parallel to Isa 65:13-15.

[10] This also recalls and corresponds to the new names given to Zion and the land in Isa 62:2-4. There is, of course, a close relationship throughout the text of Trito-Isaiah between the servants of Yhwh and Zion. Both represent the remnant that has remained faithful and is chosen by Yhwh.

[11] The passage is central to Paul Hanson's theory regarding the "Dawn of Apocalyptic" and the transition from "prophetic eschatology into apocalyptic eschatology" (Hanson, *Dawn of Apocalyptic*, 155).

Although introduced as a new unit by the opening participial clause, verses 17-25 are a continuation of Isaiah 65:1-16 as well. This is clearly seen in the pairing of the statements "the former troubles will be forgotten" (Isa 65:16) and "the former [things] will not be remembered" (Isa 65:17).[12] This memory loss with respect to the present age and its state of destruction and desolation will be occasioned by nothing less than a new act of creation. The use of the verb *br'* in the active participle form three times in conjunction with the first-person singular pronoun (twice with *hnnh*) vividly recalls the repeated use of the same verb in Genesis 1 and emphasizes this rather unique divine action. Outside of Isaiah 40–66 where the active participle of *br'* occurs eleven times, this form occurs only twice more in the Hebrew Bible (Amos 4:13 and Eccl 12:1).[13] In the non-Isaian texts, it is used as a substantive to speak of God as the Creator. Here in Isaiah, however, it has its verbal sense of imminent action, especially in conjunction with *hnnh*.

The first statement beginning "See, I am about to create" in Isaiah 65:17 speaks of a new heaven and a new earth. The middle statement in Isaiah 65:18a uses the relative pronoun rather than *hnnh* to refer to "that which I am about to create." The third and final statement in Isaiah 65:18b once again defines just what Yhwh is creating: "See, I am about to create Jerusalem." Once more Jerusalem comes to the fore in Trito-Isaiah. The new heavens and the new earth are summed up in the new city of Jerusalem. The theme of rejoicing over the newly created Jerusalem fills the rest of the chapter as it contrasts over and over again the present state with the imminent future. Now there is weeping and wailing, loss of homes and loss of goods, premature death and childlessness. Then there shall be rejoicing and delight, houses to dwell in and vineyards to enjoy, long life and enduring offspring. This passage was clearly the major inspiration for Revelation 21 and its own vision of new heaven, new earth, and new Jerusalem resplendent with joy and devoid of tears.

This passage is the last of a series of utopian visions of a future age found throughout the book of Isaiah. These appear as early as Isaiah 2:2-4 with the vision of Mount Zion as a magnet at the center of the world, drawing all the peoples of the earth toward it. Zion, Yhwh's holy mountain, will once more be mentioned as the location of this future paradise in the final verse of this chapter (Isa 65:25), and it will reappear as the final gathering place of those presently scattered among the nations

---

[12] Although verse 17 begins a new line in 1QIsa[a], there is a more pronounced break between verses 15 and 16 in that manuscript. Most of an entire line is left blank between verses 15 and 16, while verse 16 ends near the margin of the column so that a new line for verse 17 is unavoidable.

[13] Nurmela, *Mouth of the Lord*, 125.

in Isaiah 66:20. Likewise, Isaiah 11:1-9 presents a vision of future peace and well-being geographically centered on Yhwh's holy mountain (Isa 11:9). Isaiah 65:25 alludes directly to that vision with the harmony described between wolf and lamb as well as lion and ox. The significant variation on the earlier vision is the fate of the serpent, who is set apart for punishment rather than peaceful coexistence as in Isaiah 11:8. One might attempt to read the statement "and the serpent's food will be dust" as merely the transformation to a non-predatory diet paralleling the lion's eating straw in the previous line. But the allusion to Genesis 3:14 is too obvious. Being forced to eat dirt or dust (*ᶜpr*) is clearly a punishment. Furthermore, the coexisting pairs of wolf-lamb and lion-ox are borrowed directly from Isaiah 11:6-7, but the cobra (*ptn*) and viper (*ṣpᶜny*)—mentioned there in tandem with a baby and a young child—are now replaced with the isolated, dust-eating serpent (*nḥš*) from Genesis. There is thus an element that is excluded from this harmonious vision of a new heaven and a new earth. This reflects the theme of final judgment and the parting of the two ways that is so pronounced here at the end of the book of Isaiah.

ISAIAH 66

Yhwh's House and Word: Isaiah 66:1-6

Fittingly enough, the concluding chapter of Trito-Isaiah, and indeed all of Isaiah, opens with a reflection upon Yhwh's house (*byt*). The temple and its location on Mount Zion in Jerusalem has been a central point of reference and concern throughout the book of Isaiah. Yet this chapter now opens with a certain deconstruction of that centrality. In words reminiscent of the oracle of the prophet Nathan (2 Sam 7:5-7) and the prayer of Solomon (1 Kgs 8:27), the temple is relativized as being totally inadequate to house Yhwh, who transcends heaven and earth. Sacrifices, of the temple or otherwise, are mocked in a manner reminiscent of the eighth-century prophets (Isa 66:3-4; cf. Isa 1:11-13; Hos 6:6; Amos 5:21-23; Mic 6:6-7). While these verses provide a counterpoint or balance to what has been said thus far regarding the temple and Mount Zion in Trito-Isaiah (Isa 56:7; 57:13; 60:7, 13; 64:11; 65:11), it would certainly be a mistake to try to read them as simply opposed to the temple and temple worship.[1]

There are three keys to understanding the opening of this chapter. The first is the theologically astute observation that Yhwh is greater than the temple. Expressed similarly in Solomon's prayer (1 Kgs 8:27), this realization is meant not to diminish the temple (else why did Solomon bother building it?) but to remind us that God is always greater. One must resist, then, the temptation to read these verses simplistically as anti-temple. Rather, a broader and more complex picture of Trito-Isaiah's

---

[1] See Blenkinsopp, *Isaiah 56–66*, 294, and his list of commentators (including Smart, Volz, and Lau) who interpret this as a rejection of the temple and sacrificial cult. Blenkinsopp astutely points out the "confessional prejudices" that often lie behind such judgments as to what authentic worship might be. More significantly, however, he highlights the implausibility of this conclusion given the prominence and significance of Yhwh's holy mountain throughout Trito-Isaiah.

theological landscape must be painted. If Zion holds a prominent position in his theology (a conclusion that is inevitable from what we have seen), Yhwh's prominence is even greater. The power, majesty, inscrutability, transcendence, and incomparability of Yhwh Sabaoth, the Holy One of Israel, Adonai Yhwh, is a constant throughout First, Second, and Third Isaiah. It is with this Ultimate Reality in mind that even the splendor and significance of the temple must be kept in the proper perspective. The threats of placing limits on Yhwh or of falling into temple-olatry must always be guarded against.

Second, one must observe the types of sacrifices spoken of here. Dogs, humans, and swine are mentioned in conjunction with the usual sacrificial suspects. Thus, what we have here is not simply the condemnation of a hollow worship of empty ritual. Undoubtedly, Trito-Isaiah would condemn such idle lip service and "going through the motions" as do earlier sections of the book (e.g., Isa 1:11-14; 29:13). Indeed, such a condemnation of fasting disconnected from a deeper and more active faith lived out in one's everyday life was seen in Isaiah 58. But this does not appear to be the primary concern in this passage. Rather, in verse 3 we have the juxtaposition of seven active participles and their objects that provide a clue to the real issue at hand. Quite literally the first part of the verse reads:

> The one slaughtering the ox the one killing a man
> The one sacrificing the sheep the one breaking the neck of a dog
> The one who makes an offering blood of a pig
> The one who makes a memorial offering of frankincense the one
>   who blesses an idol

The immediate challenge is how to best make sense of this elliptical passage. There are two main possibilities.

The first would be to take the terms comparatively. Such an understanding is witnessed both in 1QIsa[a], which has the comparative particle unlike MT, and in ancient versions (LXX, Tg, Vg). This understanding is expressed in the RSV, NIV, and NRSV as well. The latter reads:

> Whoever slaughters an ox is like one who kills a human being;
>   whoever sacrifices a lamb, like one who breaks a dog's neck;
>   whoever presents a grain offering, like one who offers swine's blood;
>   whoever makes a memorial offering of frankincense, like one who blesses
>   an idol.

This way of reading the text would be more critical of the cultic actions in the temple, saying they are, in effect, no better than crimes, vain actions, or idolatry.[2]

---

[2] Muilenburg ("Book of Isaiah," 759) described this "complete rejection of the temple as such" as the majority position held by Wellhausen, Budde, Gressmann,

The second possibility is, by following MT, to take the terms not comparatively but cumulatively. That is to say that by juxtaposing the participles without any correlating syntax, Trito-Isaiah is not comparing these activities but listing the varied actions of one and the same subject.[3] Such an understanding is reflected in the NJPS translation:

> As for those who slaughter oxen and slay humans,
> Who sacrifice sheep and immolate dogs,
> Who present as oblation the blood of swine,
> Who offer incense and worship false gods—

This reading of the text condemns not sacrificial practices per se but the admixture of legitimate sacrifice with either immorality or idolatry.[4] Looking at the text this way, there are echoes of the unclean and idolatrous sacrifices already mentioned in Isaiah 65:3-4. Likewise, seeing the real issue not in what goes on in the temple (but rather in what is all too often associated with otherwise proper sacrifice) fits in nicely with Isaiah 61:8 where Yhwh states: "I hate robbery with a burnt offering." This second perspective fits in better with the comprehensive message of Trito-Isaiah, which preserves a prominent role for the temple on Yhwh's holy mountain.

The third and final key to understanding Trito-Isaiah's purpose at the beginning of chapter 66 is the recognition that, in addition to his

---

Schmidt, Rudolph, Volz, and Torrey, among others. Whybray (*Isaiah 40–66*, 281) sums up this perspective (which he sees as the less probable option but evidenced also in Duhm, Fohrer, and Pauritsch) thusly: "The point would then be that sacrifice of every kind is wrong, that the entire sacrificial system of Israel has from the very beginning been an offense against Yahweh." This also seems to be the interpretation of Childs (*Isaiah*, 540), although he combines to some extent the comparative (temple sacrifice is wrong) and cumulative (syncretistic sacrifice is wrong) viewpoints in stating: "In contrast to the humble and contrite (v. 2b), those who would build God a temple are the same arrogant people who defile his worship with their syncretistic, pagan cults."

[3] As Blenkinsopp (*Isaiah 56–66*, 297) states: "The first and most obvious point is that the eight [*sic*] active participles put the emphasis directly on the agents rather than on what is done or where it is done."

[4] Most commentators who analyze this perspective (e.g., Volz, Muilenburg, Snaith, Bonnard, Schoors, Whybray, Blenkinsopp) emphasize cultic offense over ethical offense. That is to say that they interpret the phrases "killing a man" and "breaking a dog's neck" as referring to sacrificing humans and dogs and not simply murder or animal cruelty. Muilenburg ("Book of Isaiah," 762) draws a cultic parallel by mentioning that in Justin's *History of the World* (19.1.10) "Darius forbade the Carthaginians to offer human victims in sacrifice or to eat the flesh of dogs." That cultic syncretism is the main concern is possible but not certain. The possibility that correct cult combined with unethical behavior (see Isa 61:8) is also an issue (if not the only issue) should not be ignored.

description of unacceptable worship, Trito-Isaiah offers a vision of authentic worship. This is expressed twice in these few verses: Yhwh desires those who tremble at his word (Isa 66:2, 5). Throughout Trito-Isaiah the wicked are characterized as those who are indifferent to Yhwh's word and will, those who do not seek Yhwh or what he desires (Isa 65:1-2). The opposite of this is found in those who "tremble" (*ḥrd*) at Yhwh's word. The distinctive phrase "to tremble at the word(s)" of Yhwh (or God) occurs only here and in Ezra 9:4.[5] Interestingly enough, the contexts in both Isaiah and Ezra speak about God's judgment on syncretistic practices (of cult or intermarriage) in the postexilic community. The trembling may be reflective of a pious fear as the divine judgment and punishment of the wicked unfolds, or it could more generically refer to that same human attitude when simply aware of the awesomeness of God (see Exod 19:16). Whatever the case may be, what is clear is that those who tremble at Yhwh's word are those who are attentive to what Yhwh desires. They are the servants of Yhwh who are also concerned for Jerusalem, Zion, and the house on Yhwh's holy mountain, for it is the very restoration and exaltation of these that the word of Yhwh has been proclaiming throughout Trito-Isaiah. Finally, if there were any lingering doubts about Trito-Isaiah's positive position with regard to the temple, Isaiah 66:6 identifies the temple as the origin of Yhwh's voice announcing and accomplishing the retribution that now unfolds in this final chapter of Isaiah.[6]

Verse 6 concludes this section with a threefold repetition of the word "voice" (*qwl*). In the first three lines of this verse, each beginning with the word "voice," we hear of a voice thundering (1) from the city, (2) from the temple, and (3) of Yhwh. The three voices are in fact one voice—that of Yhwh—identified with increasing precision in each line. The voice of Yhwh described here can be identified with the "word of Yhwh" that was mentioned in verses 2 and 5. It emanates from Jerusalem, from the temple, and ultimately from Yhwh himself. The progression in these three lines of Isaiah 66:6 is a movement toward the center of these concentric circles. Just as the temple is within Jerusalem, Yhwh is portrayed as being within the temple as the ultimate source of the thundering voice. A close connection is thereby made in these verses between the temple of Yhwh and the word/voice of Yhwh that emanates from it. The servants

---

[5] The similar phrase in Ezra 10:3—"to tremble at the commandment of our God"— clearly has a comparable sense of taking with utmost seriousness the divine utterance.

[6] Commentators who wish to maintain an absolute rejection of the Jerusalem temple in verse 3, strain to disassociate Yhwh's judgment from Jerusalem and from the temple in verse 7 (see Smart, *History and Theology*, 289).

of Yhwh tremble at this awesome word of judgment, while the rebels—the enemies of Yhwh—receive the retribution that this voice requites. The voice of Yhwh, like the word of Yhwh (Isa 55:11) is the active agent here and the subject of the Piel participle *mšllm* ("repaying" or "fulfilling"). Here is yet another allusion to Isaiah 55 with its active word of Yhwh going forth to accomplish Yhwh's will and pleasure.

Mother Zion and Mother Yhwh: Isaiah 66:7-14

True to the pattern of chiaroscuro that we have seen throughout Trito-Isaiah, before the scene of final judgment painted in dark tones appears, one last brilliant burst of light breaks forth to heighten the contrast even more. This final shining moment of joy begins with a miraculous birth announcement: "Before she labored, she gave birth. Before birth pangs came to her, she bore a son" (Isa 66:7). The unnamed mother of verse 7 is soon identified as Zion in verse 8. What is born is likewise identified in verse 8 as land, nation, and Zion's children. The imagery is quite clear, speaking of the unprecedented speed with which the national restoration will take (or has taken) place. The answers to the interrogatives in verse 8 are then found in the rhetorical question responses of verse 9. How could such a miraculous restoration happen? How could it not, as it is the work of Yhwh, your God?

The literary connections to earlier portions of Deutero- and Trito-Isaiah also stand out in this section. The returning and restored children of Mother Zion have already been mentioned in Isaiah 49:17-25 and 60:4, 9. The miraculous and prodigious birth of children to the barren and desolate one in Isaiah 54:1-3 (especially in conjunction with Isa 62:1-5 where the desolate Zion receives a new name) also echoes loudly in this passage. Even the form of the rhetorical question pointing to the incomparable activity of Yhwh is a familiar device of the latter part of the book of Isaiah (e.g., Isa 40:13, 18, 21; 41:2, 26; 43:9, 13; 44:7, etc.).

The themes of rejoicing and consolation, also so prominent throughout Isaiah 40–66, come to the fore once more in verses 10-14. The address to those who have mourned over Jerusalem to now rejoice with Jerusalem and be glad in her (Isa 66:10) repeats the now-familiar theme of mourning turned into joy from both Deutero- (Isa 49:13; 51:11; 54:1) and Trito-Isaiah (Isa 60:5, 20; 61:1-11; 65:13-14, 18-19). Indeed, this can be seen as the principal theme of the "core of core texts" (Isa 61) in Trito-Isaiah. As the prophet begins to clothe this message of joy and consolation with imagery, the initial figure represented is that of a nursing child in verse 11. Mother Zion becomes, in this way, pictured not only as the reason for rejoicing but the very source of consolation and delight. She who has been miraculously rebuilt, restored, and repeopled by Yhwh's incomparable action now is the conduit of Yhwh's blessings of consolation and comfort to her children. This dynamic is neatly expressed in verse 12, where Yhwh once again promises to give to "her" prosperity and the wealth of nations like an overflowing river, while "you" (pl.) will nurse or suck it in (*ynq*).[7]

With verse 13 the comforting mother spoken of is no longer Zion but Yhwh himself. Zion is now the location of this comforting by Yhwh. Taking verses 10-14 together, one might say that Jerusalem functions almost sacramentally as the tangible means through which Yhwh extends his blessings of consolation, joy, and comfort to his people. One can also see yet another connection to Isaiah 49:13-15 where the concern and comfort that Yhwh has for his people is compared to that of a mother toward her child. The tender feminine imagery with which Yhwh is depicted here makes for a striking contrast with the blood-stained warrior of Isaiah 63:1-6. In fact, a striking contrast can be seen by focusing on this passage alone, since in Isaiah 66:13-14 the image of Yhwh as mother is combined with that of Yhwh as warrior. Far from being a sign of inconsistency or incompatible sources or redactional layers, this is what Marc Zvi Brettler describes as "metaphorical coherence through 'contradictory' metaphors."[8] That is to say, while the imagery may be contradictory on a literal level, it comes together significantly on a metaphorical level. The combination of the metaphors of mother and warrior is actually necessary to achieve the desired portrait of Yhwh as not simply a monotone caricature but rather as "both supremely compassionate and supremely powerful."[9]

With verse 14 the rejoicing of those in Jerusalem is described as extending to both the heart and the bones. This joy is thus not limited to

---

[7] LXX understands the verb in MT as a substantive "their children," leading many commentators to emend the text to "their [or her] infants" (literally, "sucklings"). This emendation is often made on the claim that MT makes poor sense (Muilenburg, "Book of Isaiah," 767; Whybray, *Isaiah 40–66*, 285; Blenkinsopp, *Isaiah 56–66*, 304). Actually, the shifting metaphor makes quite reasonable sense as the liquid blessing flowing into Jerusalem now flows out of her to her children. The river metaphor of verse 12 is in fact bracketed with imagery of maternal nursing in verses 11 and 13. This is not the first case of Trito-Isaiah using metaphors in tandem. Furthermore, the emendation would require a further emendation of the following verbs from second to third person.

[8] Marc Zvi Brettler, "Incompatible Metaphors for Yhwh in Isaiah 40–66," *JSOT* 78 (1998): 97–120; here 118.

[9] Ibid., 119.

an interior state but is reflected in physical well-being also. The physical reconstruction of Jerusalem leads not only to spiritual revival but the material well-being of the children of Zion as well. We are also once again reminded of the source of this joy: it is the "hand of Yhwh" that has transformed our world. Yhwh's hand, the symbol of Yhwh's power, has brought about this ultimate victory. And now, in a final transition that leads to the conclusion of the book, we are reminded at the end that the hand of Yhwh wields a two-edged sword: "Yhwh's hand will be known with his servants, but a curse with his enemies" (Isa 66:14b).[10] As we speedily come to the conclusion of the book, the servants and enemies of Yhwh are set apart and contrasted once more. The former shall see Yhwh's saving power, while the latter will receive a curse as the just retribution that their actions have brought upon themselves.

The Final Judgment of All Flesh: Isaiah 66:15-24

Almost all commentators have seen in the concluding verses of the book of Isaiah a series of short and disparate sayings indicative of successive scribal activity that attempts to bring the book to a fitting conclusion. The first of these can be seen in verses 15-16 with its *hnnh* clause with the active participle marking the imminent future so pervasive throughout Trito-Isaiah. The addition of the particle *ky* is often taken by commentators as connecting these verses to the preceding section (or some earlier section), but this does not preclude recognizing this brief passage as the first of several conclusions to Isaiah.[11] The scene of theophany and judgment in these verses is marked by the threefold repetition of the word "fire" (אֵשׁ) in Isaiah 66:15-16a. This is the final usage of the triple formula that has been so characteristic throughout Trito-Isaiah, and it gives an ominous foreboding of the coming conclusion. The predominantly negative nature of the judgment is clear from the accompanying descriptions of Yhwh's furious anger, rebuke, and sword.

---

[10] The word *z⁽m* may be read as a noun ("a curse") or a verb ("he will curse").

[11] Childs (*Isaiah*, 541) considers verses 15-16 together with the more prosaic verse 17. Blenkinsopp (*Isaiah 56–66*, 307) sees verses 15-16 as having no connection to verse 17 and sees verse 16 as the original conclusion to Isa 56–66, corresponding to the original conclusion of Isa 40–54 in 54:17c. Muilenburg ("Book of Isaiah," 768–69) also sees verses 15-16 as the original conclusion, referring to verses 17-24 as the addition of a redactor. Whybray (*Isaiah 40–66*, 287) sees verses 15-16 as "originally the continuation of verse 6" as does Westermann (*Isaiah 40–66*, 421).

The remaining series of brief conclusions finds each passage clearly marked and distinguished by an indicator of divine speech—either *n'm yhwh* (Isa 66:17, 22) or *'mr yhwh* (Isa 66:21, 23). The final declaration of "says Yhwh" is then the repetition of verse 23, which has been reproduced after verse 24 so that the entire book of Isaiah bears the divine signature so to speak. Without attempting to identify the times and motives for each of these concluding oracles, we shall consider them together.

Isaiah 66:17, following the announcement of Yhwh's coming judgment with threefold fire (Isa 66:15-16), directs our attention to the targets of this coming divine rebuke. "Those who sanctify themselves" and enter "into gardens" and eat "swine's flesh" recalls the vocabulary of Isaiah 65:3-5. In fact, Yhwh's anger and the imagery of fire are also mentioned in Isaiah 65:5b-6, similar to what we found in Isaiah 66:15-16. Thus we see yet another instance of distant chiasm:

Isaiah 65:3-5a	*gnwt*	*'kl bśr hḥzyr*	*kdš*
Isaiah 65:5b-6	*'py*	*'š*	
Isaiah 66:15-16	*'š*	*'pw*	
Isaiah 66:17	*kdš*	*gnwt*	*'kl bśr hḥzyr*

The idolaters or syncretists called into judgment in Isaiah 65–66 at the end of Trito-Isaiah were also the object of prophetic denouncement toward its beginning (Isa 57:3-13).

The difficult syntax of verse 18 introduces the next prophetic utterance, which concludes with "says Yhwh" at the end of verse 21. Literally, MT reads: "But I their works and their thoughts . . ." and continues with the third-person feminine singular perfect of the verb "to come."[12] Most commentators agree that the present state of MT is unintelligible. Many, following Duhm, read the phrase "their works and their thoughts" as an intrusion from another location.[13] Some translations, such as the NRSV, follow the LXX and Peshitta in supplying the verb "know" in the opening clause: "For I know their works and their thoughts." Once we get beyond the difficult text introducing this passage, we see the confluence of many key Trito-Isian themes that make for a fitting summary conclusion.

There is the return of exiles, scattered throughout the world, back to Jerusalem and Yhwh's holy mountain. We also see the nations themselves

---

[12] Most of the ancient versions (LXX, Syr, Vg, Tg) have the third masculine singular form, while 1QIsaᵃ has the third-person plural!

[13] Duhm, *Das Buch Jesaja*, 486.

actively involved in this repatriation. The manifestation of the glory of Yhwh throughout the whole world is mentioned once more. And there is perhaps a reference to the incorporation of foreigners into the community of those who worship Yhwh in his temple on Mount Zion. There is, however, ambiguity and debate about this final point.

The most striking parallel to this passage is at the beginning of the book of Isaiah where a similar stream of peoples from throughout the world comes to Mount Zion to worship Yhwh there (Isa 2:2-4). These two dramatic pieces stand like bookends around the entire book. Isaiah 66:18-21 also strongly echoes the core of Trito-Isaiah's message in Isaiah 60–62, making it a fitting concluding summary of chapters 56–66. The question that arises when making the comparisons between these chapters is exactly how true the parallel is. Isaiah 2:2-4 speaks of "all the nations" (*kl hggwym*) and "many peoples" (*ʿmmym rbbym*) embarking on a pilgrimage to Zion. Isaiah 60–62 is more varied in describing who and what comes to Jerusalem. Principally it appears to be the children of exile, Jerusalem's own sons and daughters who are coming to Zion (Isa 60:4, 9): not "many peoples" but "your people" (*ʿmmk*) are coming to possess the land (Isa 60:21). These are called "the holy people" (*ʿm hqqdš*) and "the redeemed of Yhwh" (*gʾwly yhwh*) (Isa 62:12). What comes from the nations or peoples is primarily their wealth as tribute or spoils (Isa 60:5-7, 9, 11, 13, 17; 61:6). If the nations or peoples themselves come, it is mainly to carry tribute, escort returning exiles or serve them, or witness the glorious restoration (Isa 60:9-12, 14, 16; 61:5, 9; 62:2). Finally, it is Yhwh himself who is coming to Zion in the Trito-Isaian core (Isa 60:1-2; 61:1; 62:11).

In Isaiah 66 we may note first of all that the first "conclusion" in verses 15-16 also spoke of the coming of Yhwh, though not explicitly into Jerusalem in that brief passage. Isaiah 66:18 speaks of gathering "all the nations" (*kl hggwym*), reminiscent of Isaiah 2:2 and their coming to behold the glory of Yhwh, similar to Isaiah 60:3 and Isaiah 62:2.[14] So while the initial description of the pilgrims to Zion here in Isaiah 66 matches up precisely with that in Isaiah 2:2, the motive more closely corresponds to that in the Trito-Isaian core.[15] The conclusion thus more closely integrates the central themes and images of Trito-Isaiah with the spectacular vision of Proto-Isaiah. We may also note, in addition to the grand bookending

---

[14] In the latter passage that mentions nations seeing "your glory," the possessive pronoun is feminine and refers to Jerusalem. Yet it is worth pointing out inasmuch as the glory that Jerusalem possesses is bestowed on her by Yhwh and so in fact Yhwh's glory.

[15] The motive in Isa 2:2-4 was to be taught by Yhwh, to receive instruction (*twrh*) and the word of Yhwh (*dbr yhwh*) that go forth from Jerusalem.

between Isaiah 2:2-4 and Isaiah 66:18-21, there is an allusion back to the beginning of Trito-Isaiah (Isa 56:3-8) where foreigners were part of the larger gathering promised by Yhwh.

Verse 19 reverses the flow, with the motion no longer toward Jerusalem but from Jerusalem, as the "survivors" (*plytym*) are sent to the nations to spread abroad the fame and glory of Yhwh. The idea is the same, however. The dispersed of Israel (see Isa 56:8) whom Yhwh has brought back to Jerusalem are but the firstfruits of a larger harvest. In fact, they are now seen as the instruments through whom Yhwh will declare his glory to all the nations, prompting this second wave of migration toward Jerusalem.[16] They go out from Jerusalem in order to bring even more to Jerusalem. There is some debate as to who constitutes this second wave. Do the third-person plural pronouns in verses 20-21 refer to Israelites who are still scattered abroad, or do they refer to foreigners? In other words, is the position taken here more universalistic or more sectarian? On the one hand, the reference to bringing "all your brothers from the nations" (Isa 66:20) would seem to emphasize a further return of Israelites. On the other hand, "from them" or "some of them" (Isa 66:21) appears to refer to the nations both grammatically and logically, stating that Yhwh will also take some foreigners to be priests and Levites.[17] If we take these verses together, we may observe a progression that includes both the still-scattered Israelites and the nations.

Isaiah 66:18-19	Mission to all the nations (*hggwym* mentioned three times)
Isaiah 66:20	The nations then bring "all your brothers" with them as they come to Zion
Isaiah 66:21	Some of these pilgrims to Jerusalem (nations, Israelites, or both) are taken for priestly service

[16] One can see here a close theological connection to the role of the servant of Yhwh in Deutero-Isaiah (Isa 49:6) as the instrument who brings Yhwh's light or glory to the nations.

[17] Westermann (*Isaiah 40–66*, 423) argues for reading verse 20 as a later interpolation that attempted to transfer the identity of "them" from the nations (the final word of verse 19, which would then be the clear antecedent of the pronoun opening verse 21) to "all your brothers." Whybray (*Isaiah 40–66*, 291–92), however, points out that while both antecedents are possible in the text as it now stands, understanding "some of them" to refer to the nations makes better sense "since the whole emphasis is upon them" (p. 291).

This combining of nationalistic and universalistic perspectives continues in the next brief oracle in verses 22-23. After opening by recalling the new heavens and the new earth promised in Isaiah 65:17, the endurance of "your seed and your name" is promised (Isa 66:22). The second-person plural pronouns, which are without antecedent, are presumably addressed to the readers or hearers of the text, thus to the Israelites regathered in Jerusalem or to a subset thereof (i.e., the "servants of Yhwh"). Following a chiastic reading of the whole of Trito-Isaiah, one can see an allusion back to the name promised to the faithful eunuchs at the beginning of chapters 56–66 (Isa 56:5). Yet the endurance of Israel— their miraculous preservation and restoration to which Trito-Isaiah gives witness—is linked once more with a universalistic end. "All flesh shall come to worship before me" proclaims verse 23. The inaugural visions of Isaiah 2 and Isaiah 56, along with the core visions of Isaiah 60–62 are thus reaffirmed at the end of all Isaiahs.

"How appropriate that the book of Isaiah should end on such an optimistic and universal note," thought more than one scribe or editor involved in its composition. But the eschatological vision of a new world and its endless cycle of all flesh worshiping Yhwh month after month and Sabbath after Sabbath is followed by a final dark note focusing once more on the rebels (*pš°ym*). Here we witness the grandest inclusio and the remotest chiasm of the book of Isaiah. For surrounding the vision of the gathering of all nations to Mount Zion (Isa 2:2-4; 66:18-23) are the opening and closing judgments against those who rebel (Isa 1:2; 66:24). The parallel is tight, as the beginning and ending both speak of heavens and earth and those who have rebelled. The very opening verse of Isaiah's prophecy (after the title verse) proclaimed:

> Hear, O heavens, and give ear, O earth,
> For Yhwh speaks:
> "Children I reared and brought up,
> But they rebelled against me."

Now their final fate is declared at the end of the book, and it is a gruesome one of corpses, undying worms, and unquenchable fire.

The jarring turn of this final verse, which has no prophetic rubric of its own (as in Isa 66:17, 20, 21, 22, and 23), does not mean that it is disconnected or at odds with that which precedes it.[18] What we see,

---

[18] Whybray (*Isaiah 40–66*, 293) especially highlights the contrast between verse 24 and verse 23, arguing that the author of the final verse "was possessed by a polemical passion" evidently not shared by the earlier author of verse 23. The tendency here to dismiss somewhat the final verse as a late addition, or as a conclusion to the whole

rather, is once more the stark shadow that allows the brilliant light to be defined and seen more clearly. The final phrase of the verse—"to all flesh"—repeats the reference to "all flesh" in Isaiah 66:23. Reading the verses together, one observes that "all flesh" is in fact the antecedent and subject of the verbs in verse 24: "They shall go out and they shall see." So in one sense, the focus has not shifted to the rebels but is still on the righteous. All those who have been gathered in Jerusalem from among the nations are still the subject, while the rebels and their fate are merely the object of their gaze and abhorrence. The verb *r'h* with the preposition *b* has the sense of looking with pleasure, or triumphantly, on one's enemies (see, e.g., Ps 54:9). This is clearly the case here, where the judgment on the rebels is portrayed through the eyes of the just, not so much as the defeat of the former, but as the victory of the latter. Yhwh has triumphed, bringing victory and salvation to the righteous.

---

of Isaiah 1–66 but therefore "outside" of Trito-Isaiah proper, fails to do justice to the overall message of Trito-Isaiah. We saw the same tendency earlier in marginalizing the "problem verse" of the core of Trito-Isaiah (Isa 60:12).

INDEX OF BIBLICAL REFERENCES

2014. 12. 12   29.95